DAVID EGAN

PEOPLE, PROTEST AND POLITICS

Case Studies in Nineteenth Century Wales

GOMER PRESS
1987

WELSH HISTORY TEACHING MATERIALS (14-16)

A project funded by the Welsh Office Education
Department and based at University College, Swansea

Director: Dr. Gareth Elwyn Jones
Research Officer: David Egan

Steering Committee:

O. E. Jones, HMI (Chairman)
Alun Morgan, HMI

Ian Green
Mrs. Mary-Lynne Perren
Miss Elaine Thomas
Mrs. Peggy George

Secretary: Brian Duddridge
Secretarial Assistant: Mrs. A. M. White

Printed by Gomer Press, Llandysul, Dyfed

First Impression - March 1987
Second Impression - January 1988

ISBN 0 86383 350 0

CONTENTS

ACKNOWLEDGEMENTS

I should like to acknowledge the help and assistance of the following people who, in various ways, have made possible the writing of this book: The Welsh History Teaching Materials (14-16) Project Steering Committee and particularly its Director, Dr. Gareth Elwyn Jones; Mr. J. F. Lane and Mr. C. N. Jones of Mountain Ash Comprehensive School, Mid-Glamorgan; Mr. D. Maddox of Mid-Glamorgan L.E.A., Dr. Keith Strange and Mr. Brian Davies. My debts to a number of academic historians who have written on the incidents considered in this book will be obvious; in particular I have relied heavily on the following works: Professor Gwyn A. Williams', *The Merthyr Rising* (London, 1978); the late Professor David Williams', *The Rebecca Riots* (Cardiff, 1955); and Dr. David J. V. Jones', *The Last Rising: The Newport Insurrection of 1839* (Oxford, 1985). My greatest debts, however, are to my family— my wife Susan and my children Kate and Owen —and it is to them that I wish to dedicate this book.

David Egan

Time Lines

1. THE MERTHYR RISING 1831

March— Publication of Parliamentary Reform Bill. Merthyr Select Vestry decides to reform parish administration including Poor Law.

28 March— William Crawshay of Cyfarthfa announces wage cuts for his workers.

22 April— General Election called and beginning of 'Reform Crisis'.

9-10 May— Reform demonstrations in Merthyr.

23 May— Crawshay's wage cuts come into effect.

30 May— Mass meeting of workers at the Waun.

1 June— March to Fothergill's works in Aberdare and attack on the Company shop. At Hirwaun crowd takes back trunk of Lewis Lewis seized by Court of Requests.

2 June— Crowd marches through Merthyr recovering goods taken by Court of Requests, attacking houses and the Court. Riot Act read and troops sent for.

3 June— Troops arrive in Merthyr. Outside Castle Inn crowd moves on soldiers, who open fire to disperse crowd.

4 June— Ambushes of soldiers and ammunition at Hirwaun and Cefn Coed. March on Penydarren House breaks up.

6 June— March from Monmouthshire to join Merthyr crowd broken up by soldiers at Cefn Coed. Panic and arrests follow.

7 June— Mass return to work. Eighteen leaders of Rising taken into custody.

13 July— Beginning of trials at Glamorgan Assizes.

13 August— Richard Lewis hanged at Cardiff.

September— Lock-out of union members in Merthyr ironworks.

November— Defeat of the union and return to work.

2. THE REBECCA RIOTS

1839

13 May— First Rebecca attack at Efailwen.

6 June— Second attack at Efailwen.

7 July— Soldiers arrive at Narberth from Brecon.

17 July— Third attack at Efailwen.

23 July— Whitland Turnpike Trust removes its new gates.

1842—

20 October— Main Turnpike Trust erects new gates at Mermaid, near St. Clears.

18 November— Mermaid and Pwll-Trap gates destroyed and Rebecca re-appears.

24 November— Gates at Trevaughan destroyed.

12 December— All gates at St. Clears destroyed.

20 December— Two London Metropolitan policemen sent to West Wales.

1843—

16 January— Further attack at Trevaughan.

1 February— First attack in Pembrokeshire at Prendergast.

1 May— First appearance of Rebecca in Teifi Valley, Cardiganshire.

26 May— Gates within Carmarthen attacked.

9 June— Special Constables fired at in Blaen-y-coed, Carmarthenshire.

16 June March and attack on Workhouse in Carmarthen.

23 June— Infantry join Cavalry in West Wales.

1 July— First attack at Pontarddulais.

18 July— Attacks on Salmon Weirs in Teifi Valley.

20 July— Attack at Llangyfelach, near Swansea. Thomas Campbell Foster attends Rebecca meeting at Cwm Ifor.

26 July— Government Inquiry commences.

2 August	First appearance of Rebecca in Llanelli area.	1843—	
25 August	Mynydd Sylen meeting.	26 October—	Trial of Pontarddulais rioters at Cardiff.
6 September—	Pontarddulais Riot.	30 October—	Government Commission of Enquiry begins.
9 September—	Murder of Sarah Williams at Hendy Tollgate.	27 December—	Trial of Shoni, Dai and others at Carmarthen.
23 September—	Final attack by Dai'r Cantwr and Shoni Sgubor Fawr.		
30 September—	Final appearance of Rebecca in South Carmarthenshire.		

3. CHARTISM IN WALES

June 1836—	London Working Men's Association formed. John Frost elected Mayor of Newport.		Wales meet at Blaina and agree to rising at Newport.
April 1837	Birmingham Political Union revived.	3-4 Nov. 1839—	March of Chartists from Monmouthshire Valleys on Newport and failure of rising.
1837—	Chartist branches formed in Wales including those at Carmarthen (first in Wales), Newtown (first in Mid-Wales) and Pontypool (first in Monmouthshire).	January 1840—	Chartist trials at Monmouth Assizes. Among sentences, Frost, Williams and Jones sentenced to death for leading Newport Rising.
May 1838—	People's Charter and National Petition launched.	Feb. 1840—	Death sentences on three Chartist leaders reduced to transportation for life.
Feb. 1839—	Chartist National Convention opens in London.	1842—	Chartist revival in Britain (including Wales) in support of 2nd Petition, which Parliament again rejects. Chartist strike in South Wales.
April 1839—	Chartist disturbances at Llanidloes.		
July 1839—	Trial of Mid-Wales Chartists. Parliament rejects 1st Chartist Petition by 235 votes to 46.		
August 1832—	Henry Vincent and Monmouthshire Chartists imprisoned after trial at Monmouth Assizes.	1848—	Further Chartist revival in support of 3rd Petition which is again rejected by Parliament.
Sept. 1839—	Chartist National Convention decides on series of risings (including Newport) to achieve Charter.	1853—	Chartist revival.
		1856—	John Frost returns to Newport after a pardon, to a hero's welcome.
3 Oct. 1839—	Chartist leaders in South	1858—	Last Chartist National Conference (attended by delegates from Merthyr Tydfil and Aberdare).

4. THE TITHE WAR IN NORTH-EAST WALES

1836—	Tithe Commutation Act (tithes payable in money instead of in produce).		evicted by landlords for supporting Liberal candidates.
1859—	*Baner Ac Amserau Cymru* founded by Thomas Gee. Following General Election, Nonconformist tenant farmers in Merionethshire	1867—	Parliamentary Reform Act gives vote to working-class householders in towns.
		1868—	Many Liberal victories in Wales in General Election. Further evictions of tenant

farmers for supporting Liberals in election.

1872— Ballot Act grants right to secret ballot in elections.

1881— Sunday Closing (Wales) Act—first piece of modern law passed by Parliament dealing only with Wales.

1884— Parliamentary Reform Act gives vote to working-class householders in countryside.

1885— In General Election Tory landowners in Wales defeated by Liberal candidates. Agricultural depression begins—in North-East Wales —farmers begin to seek reductions in rents and tithes from their Landlords.

1886 Welsh Land League formed with Thomas Gee as president. Spread of Anti-Tithe Leagues in North-East Wales and beginning of distraints and auctions when tenant farmers refuse to pay tithes.

Dec. 1886— First major protest against a distraint sale at Whitford marks the beginning of the 'Tithe War' in North-East Wales.

June 1887— Riot at Mochdre during a distraint.

Sept. 1887— Disturbances and arrests at Llangwm during auction of distrained goods.

1888— Tithe disturbances spread into Caernarfonshire, Montgomeryshire, Cardiganshire and Pembrokeshire.

May 1888— Disturbances at Llanefydd during distraints leads to troops being brought into North-East Wales.

1891— Parliament passes new Tithe Act—landlords made responsible for payment of tithes.

1936— Tithes finally abolished in Britain.

Places mentioned in the text

Historical Evidence

In this book we shall study examples of popular protest in nineteenth century Wales. The author will tell part of the story. The sources will tell the rest of the story. These sources are mainly documentary, although there are also many visual and oral sources.

Documents

Documents are those written records of any period in history which survive. Everything which is written down or, more recently, typed, is a document and may be of some use to the historian. Any notes which you might write to each other are historical documents. They might, sometime in the future, be of use to a historian—if they survive. It is highly unlikely, of course, that they will survive. More important documents than those, affecting the lives of hundreds of people—or millions of people, have not survived. These papers have been eaten by rats, destroyed in floods, burned or torn up or just decayed. Out of what has survived we try to find out what has happened in the past.

Other sources

We not only have documents, or written sources, to help us build up a picture of Wales during the nineteenth century. Buildings of the time which still stand tell us a great deal about living conditions, life-style, social and religious habits for example. Any clothes, or furniture, farming equipment, Chartist weapons or even pots and pans help to build up the picture. Anything which survives from the period is of some value.

Evidence

The documents, buildings, artefacts (the name given to man-made or woman-made articles) together make up our *evidence*. This is all that remains of the past. We cannot know anything about the past if there is no evidence. It is only from what survives that we can build up a picture of the past. This is what makes *primary* evidence so important and why it is important to understand the difference between *primary* and *secondary* evidence.

Primary evidence

People studying history divide their sources of information into primary sources and secondary sources. The topic of our study is Wales in the nineteenth century. Therefore all those documents, buildings or artefacts which actually came into existence during the period we are studying are *primary* sources of evidence. That does not mean that they are all of equal value. Some primary evidence is very important indeed. For example Estate records can give us essential information about how farming was carried out and what rents were actually paid by tenant farmers. The records of Iron companies can provide important information on what working conditions in ironworks were like and the wages which were paid to ironworkers and miners. Acts of Parliament tell us what laws were passed on matters such as the payment of tithes. Not all records give us quite such detailed and 'official' information as this. Newspapers, for example, which are often used as a primary source by historians, sometimes give us only the view of the journalist who writes a report or the editor of the newspaper. Some people write autobiographies which tell us the story of their lives and the part they may have played in important events from their point of view. This kind of evidence we call *personal* or *media* evidence. The information provided by such evidence may not be as reliable as, say, an Act of Parliament. It is still very important indeed because it will at least tell us something about the person who wrote it even if it does not tell us a great deal about the topic. Sometimes it can provide us with information which, although less reliable than 'official' evidence, gives us a much clearer understanding of how people led their lives, even if it is only one person's view. These sources, therefore, if they come into existence during the period which we are studying, are also primary sources.

Secondary Evidence

This is not the first book to be written by an historian on Wales in the nineteenth century. There are many other books which have been written in our own times on different aspects of the history of Wales at this time. Such historians have built up their picture, often using primary sources. When they write down their ideas in books these books become sources of information themselves. The books which students of history write, are called *secondary* sources. In other words secondary sources are those accounts of the history of Wales in the nineteenth century which have come into existence *since* the events which are part of that history have taken place.

*   *   *

In all the sections and chapters of this book the parts of the story which the author has written are secondary sources. The rest of the story is told by other people. Most of the extracts are primary sources; some of them are secondary sources.

Many people who go on to study history as adults have the idea that primary sources are true and secondary sources are merely opinions. This is not so. Let us suppose that you write a diary of everything which has happened to you today and that it survives for a hundred years. Let us suppose, too, that in a hundred years time a historian is trying to reconstruct life in your school. Is the class register likely to be accurate? Yes, probably, within narrow limits. But the historian may want to get an idea of what people thought of their schools in the twentieth century, so he or she will use your diary. It is a primary source for the period, like the register. But now the historian has got to be very careful. He is dealing with a literary source. How truthful a picture do you think your diary would give, and how complete will the information be? It is just the same for us looking at our period. There are many useful primary sources but we have got to be very careful with them. Can you think of any reasons why people writing at the time might have deliberately set out to deceive others around them and the people who were likely to read about events later?

Case Study 1:
The Merthyr Rising 1831

1. Introduction

On 1 June 1831 at Merthyr Tydfil, the main centre of the iron industry in South Wales and the first large town in Wales' history, widespread demonstrations by ironworkers and their families took place. In the four days which followed, control of the town effectively passed from the ironmasters, businessmen and magistrates who usually held authority, to the demonstrators. It was not until 7 June 1831 that this major revolt was ended after large numbers of soldiers had been brought into the area. These events have passed into history as 'the Merthyr Riots of 1831' although in more recent times they have come to be called 'the Merthyr Rising' of 1831. When you have worked through the evidence in this case-study, hopefully, you will be able to see why the events of June 1831 in Merthyr Tydfil have been called both these things and perhaps you will be able to decide for yourself how they are best described.

It is also a major purpose of this case study to introduce the whole idea of 'cause and consequence' in history i.e. what appear to have been the causes of the events of 1831 in Merthyr as we understand the evidence of them. Section 2 is concerned with such causes. It will consider the tremendous growth of Merthyr Tydfil from the middle of the eighteenth century to become, by the end of that century, the fastest growing area in Wales. In particular it looks at the growth of the local iron industry which made all this possible, the importance and power of the ironmasters who owned this thriving industry and the conditions of life and work of the people of Merthyr. We will then move on to find out about outbreaks of working-class protest in the period before 1831 and how as a centre of Radicalism, Merthyr developed a reputation as a place of advanced political ideas.

Section 3 begins by considering what may have been the more immediate causes of the Rising of 1831—in particular the effect of a depression in the iron industry and the growth of political and trade-union movements. Then the events of 1831 themselves are concentrated upon and considered as 'the consequences' of what was studied in the second section. Having looked closely at the events of June 1-7, 1831, as they unfolded in Merthyr, the aftermath of these events is briefly considered. On 7 June, twenty-eight of the Merthyr demonstrators were arrested for their part in the revolt and they were later brought to trial. Four men were transported to convict colonies for the rest of their lives having been found guilty of playing a major part in events at Merthyr. One man, Richard Lewis (or 'Dic Penderyn' as he was better known), was sentenced to death for attacking a soldier with a bayonet. He protested his innocence of this charge, but despite efforts to have him reprieved, on 13 August 1831 he was hung at Cardiff. Some of the evidence on Dic Penderyn's part in the Rising of 1831 at Merthyr Tydfil, is studied as a means of considering whether he was the 'Martyr' he has been claimed to be.

2. Background to the Rising

THE GROWTH OF MERTHYR TYDFIL

From Rural Village to Industrial Town

In 1723 a traveller from England visiting the district around Merthyr Tydfil described it as follows:

Source 1

A most agreeable vale opening to the south, with a pleasant river running through it called the Taafe . . .

Source: Daniel Defoe. *A Tour Thro' The Whole Island of Great Britain*, 1724-5.

This kind of scene would have been repeated all along the heads of the river valleys which cut through the mountains of the counties of Glamorgan and Monmouthshire—the area that today we know as the 'Heads of the Valleys.' Merthyr was a small village which had grown up in an area where the Romans had built a fort (at Penydarren) and the Normans later had constructed a castle (at Morlais) to warn them of attacks by the Welsh from the north. By the sixteenth century a few scattered farmhouses around a church and a corn mill made up the hamlet of Merthyr Tydfil. The vast majority of the local population of a few hundred people earned their living from the land, keeping sheep and cattle.

A little less than one hundred years after Daniel Defoe's visit (Source 1), two lawyers from London visited south Wales. When you read their description below of the journey they made up the Taff Valley from Pontypridd to Merthyr Tydfil, you will see that great changes had taken place in that time. The print which follows, of the Penydarren Ironworks in 1813, was perhaps the dramatic scene they came upon:

Source 2

. . . About five miles from Merthyr, we saw . . . a faint glimmering redness . . . as we advanced it became more fixed with occasional deeper flashes . . . Everything was in utter darkness heightened by a thick wet fog. The road was miserably bad and dirty . . . we could now see men moving among the blazing fires, and hear the noise of huge hammers, clanking of chains, whiz of wheels, blast of bellows, with the deep roaring of the fires . . . The effect was almost terrific when contrasted to the pitchy darkness of the night . . .

Source: Tour by W. and S. Sandys, October 1819. National Library of Wales, Cwrtmawr Manuscripts.

Source 3

Source: The Penydarren Ironworks 1813. National Museum of Wales.

It was of course the beginning of large scale industry and in particular the development of the Iron industry which had so transformed Merthyr. The map below shows other areas of South Wales where by the early nineteenth century, the iron, tinplate and copper industries had established themselves.

The Growth of Population

Nowhere, however, in South Wales, had the growth of industry taken place on the scale that it had in Merthyr Tydfil. By 1831 Merthyr Tydfil was not only Wales' first completely

Source 4

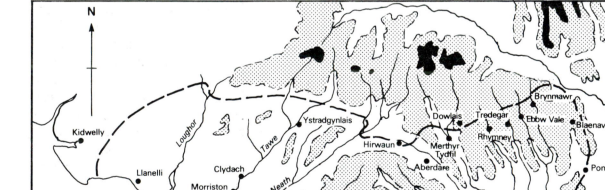

Map showing Industrial Centres in South Wales in the early nineteenth century.

industrial town, it was also far and away the largest town in Wales' history. Its population of a few hundred in the early eighteenth century had grown to 7,000 by 1801 (when the first population census in Britain was taken) and by 1831 to a total of 30,000. An increase in population was taking place in all the Welsh counties at this time and particularly so in the new industrial centres of South and North Wales. However, as the following figures show it was in the counties of Glamorgan and Monmouthshire that this increase was most marked and within Glamorgan it was Merthyr Tydfil which was the pacesetter:

Source 5
POPULATION INCREASE IN WALES 1801—1851

Welsh Counties

County	1801	1851
Monmouthshire	45,568	157,418
Glamorgan	70,879	231,849
Carmarthenshire	67,317	110,632
Pembrokeshire	56,280	94,140
Cardiganshire	42,956	70,796
Breconshire	32,325	61,474
Radnorshire	19,135	24,716
Montgomeryshire	48,184	67,335
Flintshire	39,469	68,156
Denbighshire	60,299	92,583
Merioneth	29,506	38,843
Caernarvonshire	41,521	87,870
Anglesey	33,806	57,327

Some Glamorgan Parishes

Parish	1801	1851
Merthyr Tydfil	7,705	46,378
Swansea	6,831	24,902
Aberdare	1,486	14,999
Llangynwyd (Maesteg)	806	5,479
Aberavon	275	2,380
Cadoxton	3,482	7,314
Ystradgynlais	993	3,758
Ystradyfodwg (Rhondda)	542	1,998
Llanwonno (Cynon)	426	3,253
Glyncorrwg	234	439

Source: Figures from Official Census Returns 1801 and 1851.

Although there was some natural increase in population (more people were being born than were dying) the main factor in the tremendous growth of industrial areas like Merthyr Tydfil was that thousands of people moved into them to find work in the new industries. Most of the people who came to Merthyr moved fairly short distances from the rural parts of Glamorgan and

other came from a similar background in west Wales, with a few migrating from as far as the north Wales counties. Although skilled and unskilled workers also came from England and Ireland, the 'new' population of Merthyr was overwhelmingly Welsh (the 1841 Census found that only 9% of people in the town came from outside Wales). The two lawyers we came across in Source 2 were forcibly struck by the 'Welshness' of the town as they describe here:

Source 6
They were all talking the Welsh language which sounded very strange to our ears; we could imagine ourselves to be in a foreign country amidst a distinct race . . . We did not understand them, and could scarcely get them to understand us, and they stared as if we had come from the North Pole.
Source: Tour by W. and S. Sandys, October 1819. National Library of Wales, Cwrt Mawr Manuscripts.

Culture and Religion

From the Welsh countryside the people of the 'new' Merthyr Tydfil brought not only their language, but their customs, traditions and religious beliefs. Sports such as foot-racing and fist-fighting, festivals such as the Cwrw Bach (where people drank, sang and generally entertained themselves), and local eisteddfodau all flourished in the growing town of Merthyr. Public houses were at the centre of this cultural and social life. In 1847 it was noted that there were 200 pubs or beer shops in the village of Dowlais alone. Why would public houses and drinking have been so popular in a town like Merthyr? Although at first the churches and chapels seem to have not been against pubs (they often used them for meetings) the reputation which Merthyr got for drunkenness and fighting did eventually turn the religious bodies against them.

The newcomers to Merthyr Tydfil were firmly Nonconformist. In the sixteenth century the church in Britain had broken away from the Roman Catholic Church, and, in what is known as the *Reformation*, the Church of England was set up. Some members of the new Church (including groups such as the Puritans and Quakers) did not believe that the break with the Catholic Church had been complete enough and wished to see further reforms to change the practices and teachings of the Church of England. These groups (known as 'Dissenters' or 'Nonconformists') had support

Source 7

Source: National Museum of Wales.

in the tiny village of Merthyr Tydfil where in 1690 they set up their own chapel at Cwm-y-Glo. In 1747 this chapel split and a group known as the *Unitarians* set up their own chapel at Hen Dy Cwrdd, Cefn Coed. When in the second half of the eighteenth century people began to pour into the growing irontown of Merthyr Tydfil, it was in these chapels rather than in the local church that they worshipped. The reasons why this happened are complicated. Many were Nonconformists already. The Church was dominated by wealthy land-owners and industrialists, whereas ordinary people attended Chapels. Another important reason was that the Church did not respond quickly enough to the growth in population by building new places of worship, whereas the rate of Chapel building at this time was tremendously fast. It has been calculated that by the early nineteenth century there were eight times the number of Nonconformist or Chapel members in Merthyr than there were members of the local Church of England. Not everyone, by any means, belonged to a chapel or the church, but the influence of religion and religious bodies (especially the chapels) on people's lives in Merthyr was very great.

This influence was achieved in part through the Sunday Schools and Day Schools which provided the people of Merthyr with the little formal education which they received at this time and through cultural events such as the *Eisteddfod* which played an important part in the social life of the area. Also at a time when ordinary people had very little say in their own lives (they had no political rights such as the right to vote) the Chapels—especially the Unitarians—encouraged them to join in the running of their religious bodies.

Impressions of Merthyr

The illustration above of Merthyr Tydfil in the early nineteenth century shows something of the layout of the town. Below is a map of the town in 1828. What can be seen about the way the town has developed?

Source 8

Source: Greenwood's Map of the South-East Circuit of Wales; 1828. Glamorgan Archive Service.

Although there was a road and canal linking Merthyr to Cardiff when these two Sources were created, Merthyr was still a fairly isolated place. This map of 1833 (Source 9) gives some indication of this:

Source 9

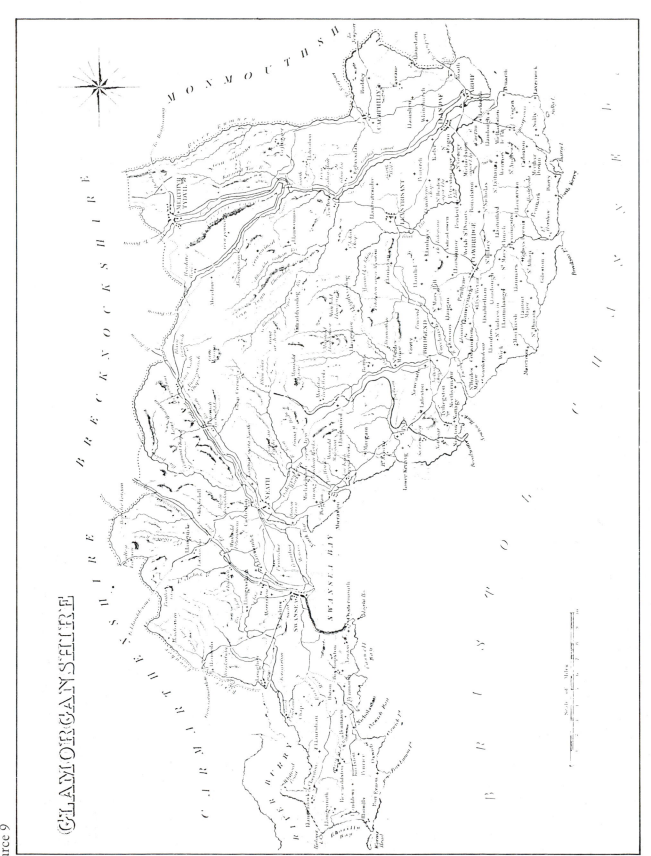

Source: Lewis's Topographical Dictionary of Wales; 1833.

Another striking feature about the nature of Merthyr at this time was the extent to which the iron industry dominated the life of its people. The table below (taken from the 1831 Census Report) gives details for the occupations of men over twenty in a number of areas in Glamorgan, including the parish of Merthyr Tydfil. Look closely at the figures for Merthyr in the table and then answer the questions to understand this domination:

Source 10

COUNTY OF GLAMORGAN

1	2	3	4	5	6	7	8	9	10	11	12	
	AGRICULTURE								MALE SERVANTS			
Males Twenty Years of Age	Occupiers employing labourers	Occupiers not employing labourers	Labourers employed in agriculture	Employed in Manufacture or in making manufacturing machinery	Employed in retail trade or in handicraft as Master or Workers	Capitalists, Bankers, Professional and other Educated men	Labourers employed in labour not Agricultural	Other males 20 years of Age (except servants)	20 Years of Age	Under 20 Years	Female Servants	PARISHES TOWNSHIPS ETC.
22	1	4	15	—	2	—	—	—	—	—	2	VAN
215	8	3	10	25	107	6	24	29	3	—	45	ENERGLYNN
182	5	8	10	15	58	3	78	5	—	—	16	GLYN-TAFF
83	8	11	13	—	14	—	21	16	—	—	8	HENDREDENNY
37	10	6	17	—	2	2	—	—	—	—	18	PARK
209	6	18	45	—	44	3	67	25	1	—	28	RHYD-Y-BOITHAN
245	3	13	5	—	28	8	178	10	—	—	21	BRITHDIR
150	10	13	10	5	21	4	78	7	2	—	34	CEFN
33	1	12	1	—	3	—	16	—	—	—	10	GARTH-GYNYD
74	10	7	11	—	19	—	22	3	2	—	24	HENGOED
28	4	7	4	—	4	—	6	2	—	—	16	YSGWYDDGWN
188	10	8	13	—	33	6	118	—	—	—	14	GARTH
84	6	11	8	—	8	—	26	25	—	—	21	GLYN-RUMNEY
60	1	—	6	7	14	—	32	—	—	—	5	RHYDGWERN
6,528	31	28	158	1,342	1,270	143	3,418	90	48	9	251	MERTHYR TYDFIL
87	7	5	28	—	8	—	14	3	—	—	27	LLANNEDOW
96	10	13	48	—	8	—	14	3	—	—	—	RUDRY
318	19	2	79	90	52	16	46	11	3	—	54	WHITCHURCH
8,639	150	169	481	1,484	1,695	192	4,144	261	63	9	594	

Source: 1831 Census Report.

1. How many are employed in agriculture? Roughly what percentage of males over twenty is this?

2. How many are employed in industry (you will need to add columns 5 and 8 to get this)? Roughly what percentage of males over twenty is this?

3. What percentage of males over twenty are to be found in column 7?

4. What kind of occupations would be included in column 6?

THE IRON INDUSTRY AND ITS MASTERS

Natural Resources and The Welsh Iron Industry

A visitor to South Wales in 1803 noted the following about the area:

Source 11

What distinguishes (marks out) and enriches this country above all the rest, is the profusion (richness) of coal, iron and limestone, which everywhere abounds. The earth . . . seems to be full of everything necessary to the use of man. Manure, metal and the means of manufacturing that metal, are all found on the same spot . . . the rivers . . . afford (give) an ample supply of water for all the purposes of life.

Source: Benjamin Heath Malkin. *The Scenery, Antiquities and Biography of South Wales;* 1807.

Source 12

Source: Tintern Furnace, National Museum of Wales.

The Romans were probably the first people in Wales to use the iron ore resources mentioned by Malkin. By the sixteenth century throughout Wales (including Merthyr Tydfil) there were small iron furnaces producing iron for local use. Large amounts of charcoal (timber) were needed to smelt the iron ore. Why would this lead to the furnaces being scattered throughout Wales? Source 12, page 8, is a print showing the furnace at Tintern in Monmouthshire. What other essential raw material mentioned in Source 11 would be nearby?

Eventually the rising price of timber encouraged ironmasters to find another fuel for smelting. Coal was an alternative but it was not until the early eighteenth century that Abraham Darby at Coalbrookdale in Shropshire, found a way of removing sulphur from coal (by turning it into coke) so that it could be used to smelt iron ore without weakening the metal produced. Therefore South Wales was to have a great attraction for ironmasters opening new furnaces. By looking back at Source 4 and particularly noticing where most of the new centres of industry developed, it should be possible to work out what this was. Along the head of the South Wales valleys from the middle of the eighteenth century a chain of ironworks were opened. The map below shows the location of the main works:

Source 13

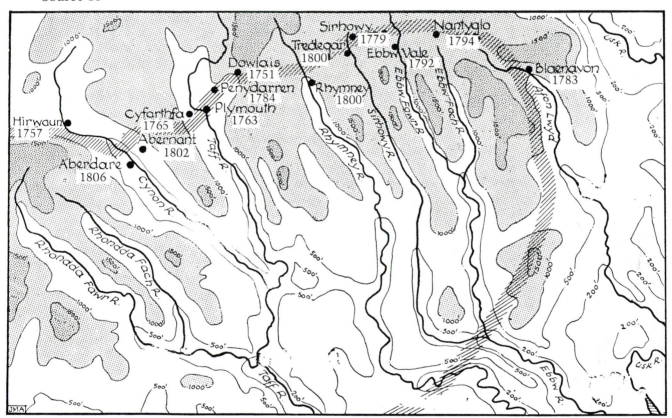

North-Eastern Rim of the South Wales Coalfield Showing Main ironworks and Date of their Foundation. Shaded Area shows the Boundaries of the Coalfield.

The Merthyr Works and Their Markets

By the end of the eighteenth century Merthyr Tydfil with its four great ironworks of Cyfarthfa, Dowlais, Penydarren and Plymouth, was at the centre of this development. The Dowlais works was started by a partnership of nine men and by 1767 the connection of the Guest family with the works began when John Guest became its manager. Under his guidance followed by that of his son and grandson, the Dowlais works expanded to become one of the largest in the world. Source 14 is a painting of the works from 1840.

Source 14

Source: G. Childs painting of Dowlais Ironworks 1840; National Museum of Wales.

Penydarren (shown in Source 3) was developed by the Homfray family until 1813 when it was taken over by William Foreman and Alderman Thompson. The Plymouth works were first developed by Anthony Bacon and then by the Hill family. Bacon had also founded the Cyfarthfa works which eventually were taken over by the Crawshay family. The expansion of the Cyfarthfa ironworks is described below by a visitor to them in 1803 and this is followed by an artist's impression of the works in 1811:

Source 15
The number of smelting furnaces at Merthyr Tydfil is about fifteen, six of them belonging to the Cyfarthfa Works . . . which are now by far the largest in the kingdom; probably indeed the largest in Europe; and in that case, as far as we know, the largest in the world . . . employing constantly upwards of two thousand men. At present more than two hundred tons of iron is sent down the canal weekly to the port of Cardiff, whence it is shipped off to Bristol, London, Plymouth, Portsmouth . . . America . . . Around each of the furnaces are erected forges and rolling mills for converting pig into plate and bar iron . . .

Source: Benjamin Heath Malkin. *The Scenery, Antiquities and Biography of South Wales;* 1807.

Source 16

Source: Cyfarthfa Ironworks 1811. J. G. Wood, *The Principal Rivers of Wales;* 1813.

By 1823 Welsh ironworks produced 43% of Britain's manufactured iron and the Merthyr works made anything from a third to a half of the Welsh output. The following figures show the number of tons sent by the Merthyr works to Cardiff for export in 1796 and 1830. What do they suggest about the growth in production from the Merthyr works and their relative importance?

Source 17

Tonnage sent by Merthyr Ironworks to Cardiff for Export

Works	1796	1830
Cyfarthfa	7,204	19,892
Dowlais	2,800	27,647
Penydarren	4,100	11,744
Plymouth	2,200	12,117

Source: Cited in K. Strange. The Condition of the Working Classes in Merthyr 1840-1850; University of Wales Ph.D. 1982.

In the second half of the eighteenth century most of this iron went to the British army and navy to make cannons and other armaments, for the country was involved in a series of wars against foreign powers for much of the period. At the end of the Napoleonic Wars against France in 1815, however, a long period of peace followed and the iron industry therefore suffered a depression. This lasted until the late 1820s and the early 1830s when the spread of railways in Britain created a new and flourishing demand for South Wales iron. Other uses for Merthyr's iron included making industrial machinery, colliery tramroads and especially supplying the many tinplate works which grew up in South Wales.

Transport and Coal

Much of the iron produced in the Merthyr works went to markets outside South Wales, and from an early date transport was important in the growth of the industry. It was the opening of the Glamorgan Canal from Merthyr Tydfil to Cardiff in 1794 which marked the beginning of the great contribution of this means of transport to overcoming the problem of moving heavy loads of iron. Each barge could carry 24 tons of iron and needed only one horse, a man and a boy to attend it. Previously such a load would have needed 12 wagons, 48 horses, 12 men and 12 boys to take it by road from Merthyr to Cardiff. The arrival of the first barges in Cardiff is described below and a graph showing the amounts of iron sent down by the Merthyr works between 1818 and 1840 follows:

Source 18
Cardiff, Feb. 13, 1794. The canal in this neighbourhood is completed, and last Friday a fleet of canal boats, from Merthyr Tydfil, laden with the produce of the iron works there, arrived at this place, to the great exultation (rejoicing), as you may imagine, of the town. With the iron treasures of the hills, we hope to grow daily more truly rich than the Spaniards are with their mines in Mexico and Peru . . . The first barge that arrived at Cardiff was finely decorated with colours . . .
Source: The Gentleman's Magazine; February 1794.

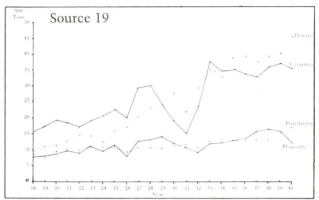

Source 19

Iron carried by Glamorgan Canal for the Merthyr Ironworks 1818-1840.
Source: 'Industrial Developments to 1918' in Merthyr Teachers Centre, *Merthyr Tydfil: A Valley Community*; 1981.

The mining of coal also thrived as a result of the tremendous expansion of the iron industry. A great deal of coal was needed to smelt iron—in the 1830s—3¼ tons for each 1 ton of iron. It was this demand for coal from the ironworks which played the major part in the development of the coal industry in South Wales up to the 1860s. Most of the new collieries opened were in fact not really separate concerns at all for they were owned and developed by the Iron Companies. The map below shows the various coal and iron ore mines which served the needs of the Merthyr ironworks up to 1860:

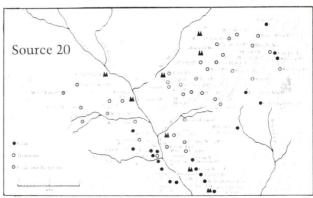

Source 20

Source: C. Thomas, 'Industrial Development to 1918' in Merthyr Teachers Centre, *Merthyr Tydfil: A Valley Community*; 1981.

The Ironmasters

Through their control of ironworks, mines and canals the ironmasters of Merthyr Tydfil became wealthy and powerful men. Most of these men were Englishmen who had moved to South Wales to take advantage of the natural resources of the area. In a speech he made in 1843 William Crawshay described how his grandfather, Richard Crawshay, (who is shown in the portrait which follows) came to Merthyr in 1786 to take control of the Cyfarthfa works:

Source 21

My grandfather was the son of a respectable farmer at Normanton in the county of York. At the age of sixteen, father and son differed . . . and my grandfather . . . left Normanton for London and rode his own pony up . . . He found employment at an iron warehouse . . . his master assigned to him the privilege of selling flat-irons, the things with which our shirts are flattened. By honesty and perseverance . . . my grandfather came into possession of this cast-iron business in London . . . In the course of time my grandfather left his business there, and came down here . . . to Cyfarthfa . . .

Source: C. Wilkins, *The History of Merthyr*, 1867.

Source 22

Source: Portrait of Richard Crawshay, Cyfarthfa Castle Museum.

Eventually, the Crawshays, by re-investing their profits, owned not only the largest ironworks in the world at Cyfarthfa, but also the George Yard Company in London (where Richard Crawshay had worked before coming to Merthyr), the Hirwaun ironworks and a tinplate works at Trefforest. Below are details of some of the profit they made at these various concerns between 1820 and 1829:

Source 23

Profits at Crawshay Works 1820-1829

Year	Cyfarthfa	Hirwaun	George Yard
1820	£15,604	£2,621	—
1821	£ 2,995	£ 107	£10,000
1822	£10,926	£196 loss	—
1823	£25,981	£48 loss	—
1824	£25,124	£ 467	—
1825	£56,154	£7,531	£43,000
1826	£27,009	£2,888	—
1827	—	—	—
1828	£15,734	—	—
1829	£ 6,540	—	—

Source: Cyfarthfa Papers, National Library of Wales.

Not all their profits were re-invested, however. In 1825 William Crawshay had a castle built as his new home at Cyfarthfa Park near to his works at a cost of £25,000. The way in which the castle dominated the town can be seen in the print of Merthyr in 1831, Source 24 *(See page 13)*. Source 25 is a description of some of the features of the castle.

Source 25

Mr. Crawshay has lately built a castle for his own residence in the vicinity of the works, which covers an area of 174 square feet, and contains 72 apartments. The locks and hinges alone cost £700. There is a pinery allocated to the castle which is heated by steam and cost £850, an extensive grapery also, that cost nearly as much.

Source: Mechanics Magazine, 1830.

Not all the Merthyr ironmasters lived as lavishly as the Crawshays, but all of them used their wealth to build fine houses near to their works and country mansions away from Merthyr. Their houses and their lifestyles contrasted greatly with those of their workers, but they did involve themselves in the life of the town. This was in contrast to the great landowners of Glamorgan who usually lived well away from the estates they rented out to their tenants. The Guests, for example, built schools, chapels and a library for their workers.

Source 24

Source: National Museum of Wales.

Returning to the Crawshays, however, perhaps the most famous example of the way the Crawshays proudly displayed their power and wealth was in 1846 when William Crawshay gave a ball to celebrate the marriage of his son. Not even the castle was large enough for this and so one of the wagon sheds at the Cyfarthfa works was used. A print of the time shows the scene at the ball:

Source 26

Cyfarthfa Ball 1846.
Source: Cyfarthfa Castle Museum.

ASPECTS OF WORKING-CLASS LIFE IN MERTHYR

Introduction

This chapter looks at some aspects of the life of the working people of Merthyr. Ideally the Sources used here should have been created by these people, but in fact there is very little of this type of evidence. Why would this be so? The evidence used is that collected by various investigators and visitors who came to investigate aspects of life in Merthyr. Most of this evidence was collected in the 1840s and 50s, but it is likely that conditions had changed very little from the period immediately before 1831.

Work and Working Conditions

It was *work* which had created Merthyr Tydfil and *work* certainly dominated the life of its people. Most ironworkers worked 12 to 13 hour shifts, seven days a week, all year round with the only official holidays being Christmas Day and Good Friday. Before looking at some of the work and working conditions of Merthyr's ironworkers, it will be useful to start with a summary of the main stages in the manufacture of iron; these were:

1. The raw materials (iron ore, coal and limestone) would be mined locally.

2. The raw materials were fed into a blast furnace (the 'blast' was hot air fed into the furnace to raise the temperature needed for smelting) where the coal smelted the iron ore and the limestone helped the liquid metal to *flux* or congeal.

3. The liquid metal would be drained off from the furnace and allowed to harden. It was then taken to the forges and mills where it was treated to further harden it before it was manufactured into various shapes and sizes.

Iron ore (or ironstone as it was often called) and coal were often mined from the same pits. The workers who mined the ironstone were called miners and those who hewed the coal were known as *colliers*. The mines were not very deep and the minerals were won by out-cropping (opencast), bell-pits or drifts (called slants and levels). This diagram should help to show what these methods involved:

Source 27

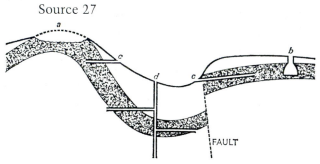

Types of coal-mining activities. Coal measures are shaded. a = Open-cast excavation ; b = bell pit ; c = drift mines ; d = deep mines with shaft and galleries.

Source: R. A. Buchanan. *Industrial Archaeology in Britain*, 1972.

Below is an account of the work and working conditions of an ironstone miner and it is followed by a description of the work carried out by door-boys (who opened and closed ventilation doors to control the air flow under-ground) in a Merthyr coalmine. The illustrat-ions which follow show children working underground as hauliers (moving the mineral to the bottom of the shaft, ready to be wound up) and a door boy:

Source 28

The roof descended so low that we had to advance in a stooping posture . . . The close-ness and heat of the pit . . . increased and the difficulty of breathing was aggravated by thick clouds of sulphurous smoke from the blasting of the rock with gunpowder . . . The miner was boring the solid rock with a long iron chisel and . . . a heavy iron hammer . . . In this hole . . . he laid a short train of gunpowder . . . In a few seconds the explosion happened . . . a gush

of smoke and flame and about a ton of stone rubbish had been displaced, leaving the vein of ironstone . . . With his crowbars and wedges he began to break this down and place it in the trams for removal . . .

Source: *The Morning Chronicle Reports on South Wales*, 1850.

Source 29

I started work when I was seven. I get very tired sitting in the dark by the door so I go to sleep. Sometimes when I am hungry I run home for some bread and cheese. Nearly a year ago there was an accident and most of us were burned. It hurt very much because all the skin was burned off my face. I couldn't work for six months. I have seven brothers and sisters . . . None of us have ever been to school.

Source: Evidence of 8 year old Philip Jones on his work at Plymouth Iron-works Mines; *Report of the Children's Employment Commission*, 1842.

Source 30

Source: *Report of the Children's Employment Commission*, 1842.

When the raw materials had been mined they were then brought to the ironworks. Source 31 *(See page 15)* is a print of the Blaenavon Iron-works. Why have the furnaces been built up against a hillside? Source 32 is a description of the smelting process.

Source 32

The furnaces generally require twelve hours for complete fusion, during which time the furnace is supplied with fresh quantities of ore and limestone . . . For the purpose of augmenting (adding to) the head of the furnaces . . . a strong blast of air is forced from a cylinder by means of a piston . . . by the arm of a steam engine . . . At the end of twelve hours

Source 31

Source: Blaenavon Ironworks, 1820. National Library of Wales.

the charge (the liquid iron) is let out into moulds made in sand troughs and suffered (allowed) to cool . . .

Source: Description of smelting process at Penydarren Ironworks. Clutterbuck's Tour through Glamorgan 1799; Cardiff Central Library Manuscripts.

The third stage of manufacturing iron involved various processes including *puddling*, *shingling* and *rolling*, to harden and shape the metal. The men who carried out this work were skilled workers, who were proud of their skills. Three sources follow. The first shows shingling (hammering the iron to remove impurities), the second rolling (to harden and shape the metal) and the third reminds us that children also worked in the ironworks as labourers alongside the skilled men.

Source 33

Source: J. C. Ibbetson. *Working Iron at Merthyr Tydfil*, 1772. Cyfarthfa Castle Museum.

Source 34

Source: The Rolling Mills, Merthyr Tydfil, c. 1817. National Museum of Wales.

Source 35

I have been working here for two years. I used to work at the squeezing machine, straightening bars of iron. I work for twelve hours a day for one week, then twelve hours a night for the next week. The work is very hard and I get tired but my dinner gives me strength . . . Sometimes I get burned at the furnace.

Source: Evidence of 9 year old Morgan Lewis, a 'puller-up' at the Plymouth Ironworks. *Report of the Children's Employment Commission,* 1842.

Wages in the iron industry varied from works to works and from time to time, so care has to be taken in looking at evidence on this. However, here are the average wages paid in 1839 for a twelve hour day and a seven day week:

Source 36

Wage Rates 1839

Miners and Colliers 22 to 24 shillings a week
Furnacemen   25 to 30 shillings a week
Puddlers   over 35 shillings a week
Highly skilled Men 50 to 60 shillings a week

Source: Report by Samuel Homfray to *The Times,* 15 November, 1839.

When considering the wages and working conditions of ironworkers at this time it is important to remember that iron workers worked slightly less hours than agricultural labourers in Wales and probably earned anything from three to six times more in wages! What other comparisons might be made between the work and working conditions of agricultural and industrial workers at this time?

Housing

Housing could be one of these comparisons. It would seem that the standard of houses built for the ironworkers of Merthyr Tydfil was no better—and perhaps was a little worse—than the homes of agricultural labourers. To meet the tide of people who flowed into Merthyr with the development of the iron industry, houses were built as cheaply and quickly as possible and they were crammed together in the new villages which developed around the works. Sandstone (quarried locally) was mainly used for building as it was cheap and readily available. It was, however a sponge-like material which easily let in damp. Here is the evidence of a visitor to Merthyr in 1803 on the way housing was developed in the town:

Source 37

The first houses that were built were only very small and simple cottages for furnace-men, forge-men, miners . . . These cottages were most of them built in scattered confusion, without any order or plan. As the works increased, more cottages were wanted, and erected in the spaces between these that had been previously built.

Source: Benjamin Heath Malkin. *The Scenery, Antiquities and Biography of South Wales,* 1807.

Only the most skilled workmen earned enough to be able to save, so that they could actually buy their own homes. Most families, therefore, rented their houses. Sometimes the Iron Companies built cottages for their workers and rented them out. Usually, however, it was the middle-classes of Merthyr (such as shop-keepers) who rented out housing and they received high profits on their investment from the rents. Here are pictures of two examples of ironworkers' cottages in Merthyr. The first is an example of the better type of working-class housing and the second (in West Lane, George-town, Merthyr Tydfil) is an example of the cheaper housing—in this case a 'split' (or 'over and under') terrace where different families lived in each storey of a single house with separate entrances from the front and back:

Source 38

Source: R. M. Evans, *Children in the Iron Industry, 1840-42,* 1972.

Source 39

Source: R. M. Evans, *Children in the Iron Industry, 1840-42,* 1972.

In areas such as Caedraw, Pont-y-Storehouse and another called 'China' near Georgetown, which became infamous, these houses soon became slums. Here is a description of condit-ions in some of the worst type of houses in Merthyr:

Source 40

A large number of these cottages consist of only two rooms, the upper being the sleeping apartment for the family and usually, ill-ventilated. Mr. Davies, superintendent of the Merthyr police, states that in these two-roomed houses . . . there are generally three beds in the sleeping apartment, containing five or six persons. These cottages are very small, 8 feet by 10 feet, and 8 feet by 12 feet being not uncommon.

Source: Report on the Health of Towns, 1845.

Public Health

Hardly any of these houses had proper sanitation and a clean water supply. In the 1840s and 50s such conditions were to lead to waves of epidemics sweeping the town, but because of such living conditions public health was always poor. The lack of sanitation is described here by a Government investigator:

Source 41

In a sanatory point of view, the state of Merthyr is disgraceful . . . The vast majority of houses have no privies; where there is such a thing, it is a mere hole in the ground, with no drainage . . . This is the case nearly all over Wales; but, in a dense population, the consequences of such neglect are more loathsomely and degradingly apparent.

Source: Report on the State of Education in Wales, 1847.

Three years later a minister of religion described to a Government Enquiry the difficulties of obtaining water in the town, it had to be queued for at water spouts in the streets:

Source 42

During winter months there are from 6 to 8 spouts, some half a mile, some 2 miles distant, from the houses, but in summer they are often reduced to three, the remainder being dried up. At these water-spouts I have seen 50, 80 and as many as 100 people waiting for their turn . . . The women have told me that they have waited 6, 8 and 10 hours at a time for their turn, and some . . . then . . . go away without any water at all . . . Instances have occurred of children being burned to death while their mothers are waiting at the spouts . . .

Source: Enquiry Into Merthyr Tydfil, 1850.

Much of the water from the spouts was taken from the rivers, which were contaminated with waste from the Ironworks, sewage and rubbish. Not suprisingly, there was a high incidence of disease and a high death-rate in Merthyr. The death rate was particularly high among the very young—in 1813 of all recorded burials in Merthyr, 67% of them were children under 5. Scarlet fever, tuberculosis, typhus and smallpox were the main killer diseases and in 1832 the first large outbreak of cholera occurred in Merthyr, claiming 160 lives. Try to find out more about these diseases and think about what aspects of life in Merthyr made them so common.

The Truck System

Another aspect of working-class life in Merthyr which is important to take note of, was the *Truck System*. Some Ironmasters paid their workers with special coins or credit notes (known as 'truck') rather than in official coinage. These could then be exchanged for goods at shops (known as 'Tommy Shops') owned by the iron Companies. In the years when Merthyr was developing as a town it was isolated and at times food supplies and other goods were hard to obtain. For this reason the iron Companies opened shops and many of their workers welcomed them doing this. Eventually, however, Merthyr had its own market and many private tradesmen opened shops in the town. Although 'truck' was never

as widespread in Merthyr as it was in industrial towns in Monmouthshire, many of the Merthyr Ironmasters still held on to their Company Shops and paid their workers in 'truck'. Often they also encouraged their workers to receive credit at the shops and so to get into debt. What might have been their reasons for doing this? Many of the ironworkers often objected to the quality and price of goods in the Company shops. The following tables of prices at 'Tommy Shops' and ordinary 'Market Shops' in Monmouthshire in 1830 gives clues about such objections:

Source 43

Goods	Market Shops	Tommy Shops
Flour, per pack	2s. 4d.	2s. 6d.
Bacon, 4 lb.	2s. 0d.	3s. 0d.
Mutton, 2 lb.	10d.	1s. 0d.
Beef, 2 lb.	8d.	11d.
Sugar, 1 lb.	8d.	9d.
Butter, 1 lb.	9d.	1s. 0d.
Tea, 2 oz	8d.	1s. 0d.
Cheese, 2 lb.	1s. 0d.	1s. 6d.
	8s. 11d.	11s. 8d.

Source: Monmouthshire Merlin, March 1830.

PROTEST AND RADICALISM

Working-Class Protest

Long before the Rising of 1831, Merthyr Tydfil and other new industrial towns in South Wales experienced a number of working-class protests. The first widespread popular disturbance in Merthyr took place in 1800-1. As a result of poor harvests there was a scarcity of food (particularly of grain) and what was available was expensive. In September 1800 workers in Merthyr expressed their discontent by attacking the company shop at Penydarren and eventually forced local shopkeepers to reduce their prices. The protest spread to other irontowns and it took the arrival of soldiers and the arrest of many of the ringleaders before order was restored. Two of the leaders of the 1800 riot were sentenced to death in September 1800 but this did not prevent further unrest in the Spring of 1801.

This type of protest was usually violent and unorganised. Trade Unions had been made illegal by the *Combination Laws* of 1799 and 1800 and there is no evidence to show that they existed in Merthyr. This does not mean, however, that none did exist! Why might this be so? *Friendly Societies* were very popular throughout South Wales at this time. The main reasons for their popularity can be seen by studying the extracts from the rules of a Merthyr Friendly Society, below. These are followed by an account of what appears to have been the first organised strike in Merthyr—is there something here which suggests that Friendly Societies were often more than they seemed?

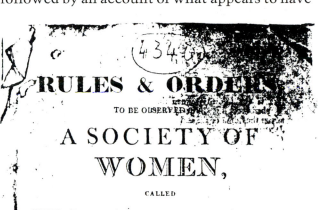

Source 44

4 'That after the expiration of one whole year from the time each member hath paid into the stock, if any member be sick or lame, and not able to work, or performing her usual or ordinary occupation, she shall have six shillings per week paid her out of the stock, until she receives all the monies she hath contributed into the funds of the said society (including premiums if any have been paid,) and for any further time or period she shall receive three shillings per week, during her lifetime, or until she resumes her usual occupation; but if such member on the attestation of one witness, be found working, or able to work or perform her usual occupation while she receives benefit, she shall be immediately excluded; and also liable to be sued for the money paid her out of the box. When any member that hath received out all her contribution, Does, there will be allowed thirty shillings towards her funeral, and a further allowance made whatever.

5 When any member of this society is grown old and unable to work, or follow her ordinary occupation, she shall have three shillings per week paid her out of the stock as long as she lives, provided she continues to pay her contribution money as other members, and thirty shillings to bury her, which shall be laid out according to the directions of the majority of this society; but if she receives three shillings per week for the term of four years her widower, friends, or relations, shall receive no further benefit from this society, or fund belonging thereto.

Rules of the Union Society
Merthyr Tydfil, 1819
Source: National Library of Wales.

Source 45

In the year 1810 the price of puddling iron was reduced from 12s. to 10s. 6d., and during the months notice it was determined by the men to resist the reduction by a strike. On the evening of the day in which the notice expired the men met by appointment in the club-room of a public house . . . Here the men took an oath . . . not to work at the reduced rate . . .

Source: Account by striker at Dowlais Works 1810 cited in C. Wilkins. *History of Iron, Steel and Tinplate Trades*, 1903.

The 1810 strike was defeated by the Guests of Dowlais, who, like the other ironmasters, refused to allow any combinations among their workmen. The ironmasters, who often competed bitterly with each other on most things, were always ready to act together to stamp out trade-unions (usually by simply refusing employment to union members) and to reduce the wages of their workers when the selling price of iron fell. This type of action by the ironmasters and their attitudes usually meant that when their workers did act against them, their actions were defensive and violent. There was no better example of this than the *1816 Strike* in South Wales. A depression in the iron trade resulted in the ironmasters reducing the wages of their workers by up to 40% and this took place at a time when the price of food was rising sharply. At Tredegar the ironworkers struck work in protest and marching gangs were sent out to the other irontowns to try and spread the action. At Merthyr Tydfil there were riots and ironworkers took over their works. William Crawshay sent the following letter to John Guest (who was in Algiers) to warn him of what was happening. This is followed by an artist's impression of the arrival of troops in Merthyr, which again was the only way the strike could be ended and peace restored to the town:

Source 46

16 October 1816, 9 o'clock by our time . . . The enemy in too great strength to oppose with any probability of success, have possessed themselves of all our Works and wholly stopped them . . . My spies tell me they threaten hard your shop, for they are hungry. I have been in the midst of them all and found as usual argument useless. I have just had a messenger from Mr. Hill. He says all his works are stopped the same as ours.

Source: Dowlais Iron Company Records, Glamorgan Record Office.

Source 47

Penry Williams, *The Arrival of Troops at Merthyr, 1816*, Carmarthen Museum.

During the 1820s the iron industry returned to prosperity and there were far fewer outbreaks of discontent in Merthyr. This contrasted with the coalmining areas of Monmouthshire, where the infamous *Scotch Cattle* were active. Although not as active in Merthyr, as the following piece of evidence shows 'the Cattle' had some support in the town:

Source 48

I was but young then, but the very mention of the likelihood that 'Scotch Cattle' were coming that night put me into a fever. The 'Scotch Cattle' were bands of men . . . with the object of restricting the output of minerals and thereby keeping up prices of iron and wages of miners. One of their laws was that no stranger should be taught mining . . . The means adopted for carrying out the rules of the Society were principally personal violence. Every herd of 'Scotch Cattle' had a bull as leader, selected for his strength and violence. The band of, say, Merthyr, was directed to punish a delinquent at Tredegar; one at Tredegar to visit Hirwaun. Each man was armed, face blackened, and the skin and horns of a cow worn, and, with great bellowings, they would assail (attack) a house, smash the furniture, and burn down the premises . . .

Source: Evidence of Merthyr resident of the 1820s quoted in C. Wilkins. *The History of the Iron, Steel and Tinplate Trades*, 1903.

Radicalism

Perhaps one of the reasons why there appears to have been little violent protest in Merthyr during the 1820s was that leaders of the ironworkers became involved in political organisations in the town. Merthyr Tydfil was from the 1790s onwards one of the strongholds in Britain of the political movement known as *Jacobinism* and *Radicalism*. The 'Jacobins' took their name from one of the most radical groups among the French revolutionaries who had overthrown the French king after 1789, for they supported their attempts to introduce more democracy into the way countries were governed. The Jacobins of Merthyr were mostly drawn from schoolteachers, writers and ministers of religion. These 'Radicals' (as they became more usually known) argued for great reforms to be made in Britain to make the country more democratic and to improve the lives of working people. In Merthyr they set up the Cyfarthfa Philosophical Society in 1806 to debate such matters and to encourage self-education among working men. Many of them were members of the *Unitarian Church*, which like other Nonconformist groups encouraged its members to educate themselves and involved them in the running of the chapels. Some Radicals went in for more violent methods of achieving their aims and the authorities were convinced they were involved in the disturbances of 1800 and 1816 in Merthyr. Source 49 is an extract from a document found near Merthyr during the riots of 1800 and this is followed by an extract from a letter found at Penydarren in 1817 just after the 1816 strike. Both are typical of the arguments which some Radicals put forward:

Source 49

There is a great many men that believes that the King has no power, but what is given him by parliament . . . it twas intended that it should be so in the beginning, but . . . he and his Ministry has got all the power . . . They ought to be deposed as well as him that has corrupted them, and a new form of government established . . . So don't lose time in . . . measures to collect yourselves together in a mass and be all of one mind as one man, and there will be no doubt of our success for the Tyrants will not be able to face us . . .

Source: 'An Address to the Workmen of Merthyr Tydfil', 1800. Published in D. J. V. Jones, *Before Rebecca*, 1973.

Source 50

Invite all that are firm and loyal to the interest of their Country, to unite . . . In Educating the human race from the wrechedness and misery that—bearly all ranks of society excepting a few privileged individuals suffer . . . Everyone are required . . . to take up arms . . . Reform . . . means that a total subversion of the present order of things must absolutely take place . . . nothing short of a revolution can save the country from ruin . . . So join hand and heart to overthrow tyranny and oppression and be a people at once free and happy . . .

Source: A letter found at Penydarren, 1817. Home Office Records.

Not all the Radicals encouraged violent revolution, however. Many of them worked for reform in the way Britain was governed rather than revolution. In the 1820s they campaigned, for example, for the abolition of the Truck System, the repeal of the Corn Laws (which they argued by stopping the import of cheap foreign corn kept the price of bread higher than it need be) and greater equality for members of Nonconformist religious groups. Their major cause was the *reform of Parliament* and in particular the way the House of Commons was elected. They criticised the fact that very few people had the right to vote in elections of Members of Parliament and argued that Britain could only be made more democratic when that right was extended to more people. They also argued that the distribution of Parliamentary seats (constituencies) was unfair to the new industrial areas of Britain where most people now lived but which had no right to elect their own M.P.s. Merthyr Tydfil was one such area. Despite the fact that by 1831 with a population of nearly 30,000 people it was the largest town in Wales, Merthyr had no M.P. of its own, yet the tiny village of Loughor in West Glamorgan with a population of just 400 could join with other boroughs in Glamorgan to elect an M.P. The town of Merthyr Tydfil was part of the county seat of Glamorganshire and only about 2,000 people in the county had the right to vote in the election of the Member of Parliament. That right came from possession of a certain amount of land and it was often the case that the great Landowners who dominated the political life of the county, were able to bribe or threaten the voters to support the candidates they wished to see elected. Thereby even the ironmasters of Merthyr Tydfil suffered, because despite all their great wealth and power it was the 'landed interests' who dominated the elections of M.P.s for the county and the interests of the ironmasters were not therefore represented. This is why William Crawshay of Cyfarthfa supported the Radicals and encouraged his workers to do the same and why all the ironmasters supported the campaign for reform of Parliament.

3. The Rising and its Aftermath

THE IMMEDIATE BACKGROUND TO THE RISING

Economic Depression and its Effects

In 1829 a fall in the demand for iron began a three-year depression in the iron industry. It led the Merthyr ironmasters to make many of their workers unemployed and to cut the wages of those still in work. Prices were rising at the time so considerable hardship resulted for hard pressed working people. In order to survive many families were forced to go into debt or to raise loans from money lenders. Often they were unable to pay off such debts. Those to whom they owed money would then turn to the *Court of Requests*. This had been set up in 1809 to allow articles such as furniture and watches to be seized by bailiffs as a way of repaying those who were owed money. With the economic depression leading to more and more poverty the activities of the Court increased after 1829 and it became more and more hated by the working people of Merthyr.

The poverty of people who were out of work, might eventually force them to claim relief under the *Poor Law*. In this age there was no such thing as unemployment or supplementary benefit and when people had no money they had to ask for help from the authorities in the parish they lived in. Each year the parish raised money from ratepayers to relieve the poor by giving them money, food and clothes. The graph below shows the effect the economic depression had on the amount of money (the Poor Rate) which had to be raised in Merthyr after 1829:

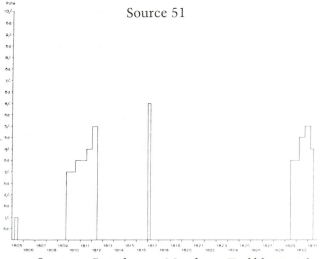

Source 51

Source: Based on Merthyr Tydfil Parish Records and taken from G. A. Williams, 'The Making of Radical Merthyr 1800-1836', *The Welsh History Review*, 1961.

The biggest ratepayers in Merthyr Tydfil were the ironmasters because, as well as their works and large houses, they owned most of the property in the town. To control the way in which their rates were spent (and whenever possible to keep down the rates raised) the ironmasters in 1822 played a part in the setting up of the *Merthyr Select Vestry*. Each year 2 Churchwardens, 4 Overseers and 20 Select Vestrymen were elected by the ratepayers of Merthyr to this body, which was charged with running the parish's affairs. By being elected themselves and by having their Agents (Managers) represent them, the ironmasters along with the shopkeeping middle-classes of Merthyr dominated the Select Vestry. The table below shows the composition of the Vestry:

Source 52

	1922	1923	1924	1925	1926	1927	1928	1929	1930	1931
Masters	4	2	2	0	0	0	0	0	0	3
Agents	1	3	7	5	4	3	3	7	5	6
Professional men	2	1	2	1	2	1	1	1	1	1
Merchants	0	0	0	0	0	0	1	1	1	0
Shopkeepers	3	3	0	2	2	2	4	0	2	0
Grocers	1	1	1	3	3	6	4	3	2	5
Drapers	1	2	1	2	2	0	2	0	2	2
Ironmongers	2	1	1	2	2	0	0	1	0	0
Tanners	0	0	0	0	0	1	2	1	1	2
Chandlers	0	1	1	1	1	1	0	1	2	0
Nailers	1	1	1	0	1	1	1	1	1	1
Innkeepers	1	0	0	0	0	0	1	0	1	0
Curriers	1	2	1	0	0	0	0	1	0	0
Saddlers	0	0	0	0	0	1	0	1	0	0
Carpenters	0	0	1	1	0	0	0	0	0	0
Shoemakers	0	0	0	0	1	0	0	0	0	0
Miners	0	0	0	0	1	0	0	0	0	0
Farmers	2	2	2	2	1	3	1	2	2	0
Unknown	1	1	0	1	0	1	0	0	0	0

Make-up of the Merthyr Select Vestry 1822-1831.
Source: Based on Merthyr Tydfil Parish Records and taken from G. A. Williams, *The Merthyr Rising*, 1978.

Notice that in 1831 the Masters moved onto the Select Vestry for the first time in some years. The main reason for this was probably because they were alarmed by the rise in the Poor Rate (shown in Source 51) and were determined to bring it down and to completely reform Parish affairs.

The Reform Campaign

The tense local situation caused by the effects of the economic depression was, by 1830, being made worse by the growing campaign for political reform in Britain. The Radicals of Merthyr organised themselves into a *Political Union* in the autumn of 1830 to lead the local reform campaign. In November 1830 they called a series of demonstrations in the town to protest against the Truck System and the Corn Laws. Local petitions were also raised and the support of ironmasters such as William Crawshay of Cyfarthfa and Josiah John Guest of Dowlais was gained. By the end of the year it was the possibility of the *Reform of Parliament* which was being most actively worked for by the Radicals. In November 1830 the Liberal Party formed a new Government in Britain and in March 1831 they kept their promise to bring a bill before Parliament to reform the House of Commons. Although there was local disappointment that Merthyr Tydfil was not to be given one of the seats in the House of Commons proposed in the Bill and although the right to vote in elections was only extended to the middle-classes, the Merthyr Radicals welcomed the bill as a step on the road to wider reforms. They were angered in April 1831, therefore, when the bill was defeated in a vote in the House of Commons. The Government decided to resign and fight a general election on the issue of parliamentary reform.

In Merthyr Tydfil, as in many other parts of Britain during this period known as 'the Reform Crisis', meetings and demonstrations were held to support reform. On the night of 9 May 1831 a huge demonstration in favour of reform took place in Merthyr Tydfil and William Crawshay describes below one of the incidents which took place:

> Source 53
> On the 9th day of May, 1831, my miners had heard that Mr. Stephens, a most respectable shopkeeper in Merthyr Tydfil, would not join me in supporting a Reform candidate for the County of Brecon . . . On that day, they, and other men, to the number of about 5,000 persons, met . . . opposite the house of Mr. Stephens and commenced speaking on the subject of Reform . . . Thomas Llewellin . . . proclaimed . . . that 'every one who was an enemy to Reform should be hung on the gallows, and he was the man to do it, free of expense' . . . about nine o'clock they again assembled, opposite Mr. Stephen's house, and commenced an attack on his windows with stones and other missiles . . . On the following day Thomas Llewellin and another ringleader . . . were apprehended . . . and committed to gaol . . . The mob . . . assembled to the extent of about 3,000 in number and openly stated

> . . . they would rescue them, and burn Mr. Stephens' house and murder him. Mr. Stephens . . . consented to their release.
> *Source:* W. Crawshay. *The Late Riots at Merthyr Tydfil*, 1831.

Crawshay's Wage Cuts

Later in the month of May 1831 yet another incident added to the growing excitement and tension which seemed to be sweeping through the town. Because of the continuing depression in the iron industry, two months earlier William Crawshay of the Cyfarthfa Ironworks had announced that he would soon cut the wages of his workers. Despite protests from all of Merthyr's ironworkers (for the other works were certain to make similar cuts) on 23 May, Crawshay introduced his lower wage rates and the next day sacked eighty-four of his puddlers. In little over a week's time the Rising in Merthyr was to take place and the view of two officers who were then to command troops in the town, on the immediate causes of the Rising are described below:

> Source 54
> . . . We find political motives to have disappeared except in name; and the partial reduction of wages in the Cyfarthfa Works, and the supposed grievances of the Court of Requests, together with other minor matters, formed the chief object of popular excitement . . .
> *Source:* Home Office Records, HO 41/10.

'The Union'

Whether the view put forward in Source 54 is right or not, there is one final factor which needs to be looked at in considering the immediate background to the Merthyr Rising. On the 30 May, 1831 at the Waun Common above Dowlais a mass meeting (reports on the size of the crowd vary between 2,000—10,000) of workers from Merthyr and the Monmouthshire irontowns was held. This was probably the largest political meeting of workers which had ever been held in Wales and it seems to have been organised as a result of the reform demonstrations on 9 May in Merthyr. Here is an account of what was discussed at this meeting on the Waun:

> Source 55
> Petitioning the King for Reform, the abolition of the Court of Requests, the consideration of their own state of wages, were equally attributed (said to be) the object, but those who

attended on our behalf could not ascertain (find) any particular point to have been considered, and the meeting dispersed without any resolution being come to . . .

Source: W. Crawshay, *The Late Riots at Merthyr Tydfil*, 1831.

How might William Crawshay, the ironmaster of Cyfarthfa, have got this information? Another report of the meeting noted that one speaker (who was described as 'a stranger') in attacking the Court of Requests, advised the crowd to act as follows:

> Source 56
> You have been petitioning Parliament several times for years and there is no notice taken of them. My plan is to bring the matter to a short conclusion and I advise every one of you to refrain from working any longer.
> *Source:* Testimony of John Petherick, Agent of the Penydarren Ironworks, Home Office Records.

This type of tactic was the policy of the *National Association of the Protection of Labour*, a trade-union which had been formed in the North of England in 1830. One of the parts of the N.A.P.L. was a 'Colliers Union' and by 1831 it was known to have set up branches in North Wales and to be sending its organisers into South Wales to do the same there. The 'stranger' mentioned by the author of Source 56 may well have been *William Twiss* the leader of the Colliers Union or one of his agents. What seems certain is that trade-unionism was again trying to establish itself in Merthyr and this too must have played some part in the background to the Rising.

THE RISING

The First Actions: 31st May and 1 June

After the workers' meeting at the Waun on 30 May 1831 events began to move much more quickly and it was *action* which now took the upperhand. On the 31st May bailiffs working for the Court of Requests visited the home of *Lewis Lewis* (known usually by his nickname 'Lewsyn yr Heliwr' or 'Lewis the Huntsman') at the village of Penderyn outside Merthyr. Lewis was a Penydarren miner who had fallen into debt and the bailiffs came to seize some of his property to meet these debts. For the first time, however, the authority of the Court of Requests was challenged. Lewis refused to give up any of his property and his neighbours

supported him in preventing the bailiffs entering his home. The Magistrate of Merthyr, J. B. Bruce, was sent for and eventually he managed to arrive at a compromise and the bailiffs took away a trunk belonging to Lewis.

The next day, 1 June, a workers' march left Merthyr for Aberdare and the ironworks owned by Rowland Fothergill. The reasons for the march and its outcome are described below:

> Source 57
> A large number of riotous persons assembled at Merthyr, and went over the hill . . . with clubs and menaces they compelled Fothergill, under penalty of his life, to sign a paper, stating that he had not declared that the miners of Mr. Crawshay were getting five shillings per week more than his own . . . They then demanded bread and cheese, and beer, which were divided to them. . . They next proceeded to the Aberdare shop . . . the shopkeeper . . . threw out of the windows all the bread and cheese he had . . .
> *Source:* W. Crawshay, *The Late Riots at Merthyr Tydfil*, 1831.

On the same day, at Hirwaun, a crowd marched to the home of a shopkeeper who had taken possession of Lewis Lewis' trunk. They took the trunk back by force and with Lewis Lewis at their head prepared to carry forward their demonstration into the town of Merthyr. Before going any further into the events which were fast developing into what became the Rising, it would be useful to look at the map of Merthyr on page 25.

The Attack on the Court of Requests: 2 June

On the morning of 2 June a large crowd marched into Merthyr along the Hirwaun road. They went from house to house and when they found goods which had been seized by the Court of Requests they took them and gave them back to their original owners. At the home of Thomas Williams (a bailiff who worked for the Court) when his wife refused to return articles taken by the Court the crowd ransacked the house and took many goods away. By the afternoon the size of the crowd had been swelled by workers who had left the Cyfarthfa and Hirwaun ironworks to join them. They marched across Jackson's Bridge to the area behind the Castle Inn where many of the tradespeople of the town lived. In particular they concentrated on the house of Thomas Lewis, one of the most hated moneylenders in Merthyr. They forced Lewis to sign a document in which he promised to repay a widow for

Source 58

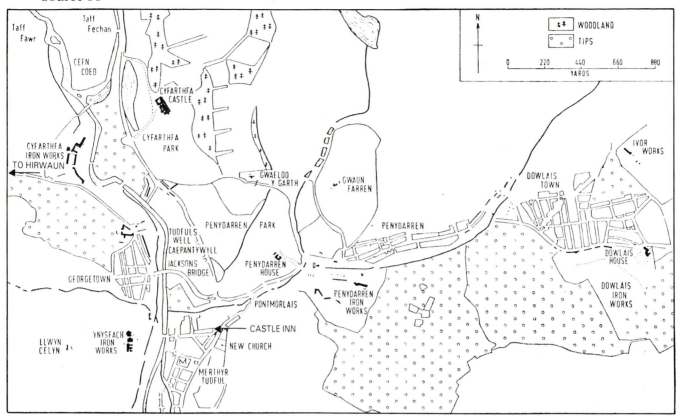

Source: Based on the Tithe Survey of 1850 and taken from H. Carter and S. Wheatley 'Some Aspects of the Spatial Structure of Two Glamorgan Towns in the Nineteenth Century', *The Welsh History Review*, 1978.

goods he had seized from her. At this point J. B. Bruce, the Magistrate, arrived. He had been taken completely by suprise at the events taking place that day, but he quickly recognised that what was happening was a widespread revolt against the working of the Court of Requests and thereby a challenge to law and order. With other magistrates (including ironmasters) he set up headquarters at the Castle Inn and enrolled about seventy Special Constables (mainly Merthyr tradesmen) to help him keep the peace. He also warned the military authorities at Brecon to be ready to send troops to Merthyr if they were needed. When Bruce arrived at Thomas Lewis' house accompanied by Anthony Hill the ironmaster of the Plymouth Works, he tried to persuade the crowd to disperse but he met with little success. Eventually he was forced to have the Riot Act read in English and in Welsh. Here is the crucial extract of what was read to the crowd:

Source 59

Our Sovereign Lord the King chargeth and commandeth all persons being assembled immediately to disperse themselves, and peaceably to depart to their habitation or to their lawful business, upon the pains contained in the act made in the first year of King George for preventing tumultuous and riotous assemblies. God save the King.

Source: The Riot Act, 1716.

Knowing that Bruce was unable to use physical force to carry out this threat, the crowd drove the magistrates away and went on to attack and raid Thomas Lewis' house.

On the evening of 2 June the crowd assembled outside the house of Joseph Coffin, the President of the Court of Requests. Here is an account of what happened there:

Source 60

They . . . demanded the books of the court, which, with all the other books in the house, were given them, and burnt in the street; the rioters then broke into the house, and dragged out, and burnt, every particle of furniture belonging to Mr. Coffin, and left the house a complete wreck.

Source: W. Crawshay, *The Late Riots at Merthyr Tydfil*, 1831.

Up to this point Bruce had been reluctant to call in soldiers, but when he heard of this attack he was certain they were now needed to put down the Rising. Troops were called from

Derby and the authorities in South Wales feared further trouble locally. Early in 1832, however, the crisis passed and the House of Lords was forced to agree to the Reform Bill which then became Law. During the passage of the Bill in the House of Commons the Government decided after all to grant Merthyr Tydfil its own M.P. for the first time. In the election for the new seat in which five hundred or so people now had the right to vote in Merthyr Tydfil, the Dowlais ironmaster, Josiah John Guest, was elected unopposed.

It might have seemed therefore that the workers' action of 1831 in Merthyr Tydfil had brought them very little result. The iron-masters held industrial power and now they had added political power to this. However, the events of 1831 in Merthyr gave rise to a new tradition of independent political activity by working people in Wales that was eventually to achieve for them many of the demands which in June 1831 had caused open rebellion in Merthyr Tydfil.

FURTHER WORK ON THE EVIDENCE

1. Look closely at Source 11 and then consider the following questions:
   a. What four raw materials needed for the production of iron are mentioned here?
   b. Explain how each was used in the making of iron.
   c. What effect did the location of these raw materials have on the development of the iron industry in South Wales?

2. Look closely at Source 16 and then try to answer the questions below:
   a. What do you think the buildings at the top left corner of the illustration were? Why have they been built close to a hillside?
   b. What stages in iron-making do you think might have taken place in some of the other buildings in the illustration?
   c. Why do you think this ironworks has been built so close to a river?
   d. Where do you think the trucks on the bridge at the right hand side of the illustration might be going?
   e. Do you think this is reliable evidence for the way ironworks in Merthyr looked?

3. Source 28 is a journalist's account of an ironstone mine in Merthyr. Read it carefully and then consider the following questions:
   a. What do you think is meant by the sentence 'The roof descended so low that we had to advance in a stooping posture'?
   b. In your own words describe what this Source tells us about the way the ironstone miner worked.
   c. What does the Source tell you about some of the dangers that were faced by miners?
   d. Do you think this is reliable evidence on work and working conditions in the mines of Merthyr Tydfil? What other evidence might be more or equally reliable?
   e. Given the date the Source was created what would you need to find out before using it as good evidence for work and working conditions in Merthyr mines before 1831?

4. The language used in Source 41 is quite difficult. By breaking up the separate points made in the Source and trying to find out what each of them means exactly, the overall meaning and inform-ation in the evidence will become clearer. So consider each of the following questions:
   a. What is meant by the phrase 'In a sanatory point of view'?
   b. What is meant by the word 'Privies'?
   c. What does the author mean when he says the conditions he describes are worse in Merthyr Tydfil because of its 'dense population'?
   d. What does the author mean when he says the consequences of the conditions he has des-cribed are 'loathsomely and degradingly apparent'?
   e. Now in your own words describe what the evidence says about conditions in Merthyr Tydfil.

5. Look carefully at Source 44 and then answer the questions below:
   a. How much were members of this Society entitled to when they were unable to perform their usual work?
   b. How much was due to a member when she was too old to work?
   c. How much would the member's family receive on her death?
   d. Source 36 and 43 give you information on wages and prices. Although they come from later dates than Source 44 they do help you to make comparisons as to what the amounts of money mentioned in Source 44 were actually worth. Look at all three Sources carefully and see what conclusions you can arrive at on the value of the benefits paid out by this Friendly Society.

6. Look carefully at Source 48 and then answer the following questions:
   a. What do you think the phrase 'restricting the output of minerals' means? Why do you think this was one of the aims of the 'Scotch Cattle'?
   b. The Source describes how men from one town would deal with 'delinquents' from

another. What do you think this means and why would it have been done in this way?

c. From the evidence given in the Source explain why those groups were known as the 'Scotch Cattle'. Why do you think they dressed and acted in this way?

7. Look closely at Source 50 and then consider these questions:

   a. In your own words describe what the author of this Source is calling upon the workers of Merthyr Tydfil to do.

   b. Do you think all Radicals would have agreed with the statement in the Source that 'Reform . . . means that a total subversion of the present order of things must absolutely take place'?

   c. What would you need to find out about this Source to make full use of it as evidence for the 1816 Strike in South Wales?

8. Look at Source 53 and then try to answer these questions:

   a. What reason is given in the Source for the first attack on Mr. Stephens' house?

   b. Explain what is meant by the statement that Mr. Stephens 'would not join us in supporting a Reform candidate for the county of Brecon'?

   c. Why do you think this Source may be biased as to the events which happened in Merthyr Tydfil on 9 May 1831? Are there words or descriptions in the Source which particularly lead you to this conclusion? What other evidence could you look for on this event?

9. Look carefully at Source 57 and then answer the following questions:

   a. What do you think the phrase 'they compelled Fothergill, under penalty of life' means?

   b. Why do you think the Merthyr ironworkers were so angry about the claim which Rowland Fothergill was supposed to have made?

   c. What do you think 'the Aberdare Shop' might have been, given that the demonstrators threatened to attack it?

   d. Who created this Source? Do you think because of this it could be biased in any way? Explain your answer and point to any words or phrases in the Source which might be evidence for what you have to say.

10. Look at Source 59 and then consider the questions below:

    a. What was the purpose of this Source?

b. Using a dictionary find out the meaning of any words or phrases you do not understand. Then re-write the Source in your own language.

c. Given the difficulty of the language in the Source do you think ordinary people at Merthyr in 1831 would have understood what it was saying?

11. Look closely at Source 65 and then answer these questions:

    a. What do you think the phrase 'contusion of the brain' means? Using a dictionary will help you.

    b. What do you think is meant by the phrase 'the bludgeons of the mob'? Again use a dictionary to help you.

    c. Why is it important to ensure that we understand what words and phrases like those mentioned above mean when we are using historical evidence?

    d. What does this Source tell us about how the disturbances outside the Castle Inn on 3 June 1831 started?

    e. Who is the author of this Source? What would you need to find out before deciding whether this is reliable evidence? What else might you look at in trying to decide this?

    f. Given who the author of the Source is do you think it could be biased in any way. Point to words and phrases in the Source which might provide evidence on this in your explanation.

    g. Bearing in mind what you have written in answer to the previous question, why do you think this Source (and the pamphlet it is taken from, which has been used a great deal in this case-study) is still valuable evidence for the events of 1831 in Merthyr? Why do you think there are no eye-witness accounts of what happened written by demonstrators?

12. Look carefully at Sources 72, 73, 74 and 76 and then consider these questions:

    a. What incident do these Sources deal with?

    b. Do you think they are reliable evidence for this incident? Explain your answer.

    c. In what respect do Sources 72, 73 and 74 agree on what happened to Donald Black?

    d. How does Source 72 differ from Sources 73 and 74 on the question of *who* stabbed Donald Black with his bayonet?

    e. What light does Source 76 throw on James Abbot's evidence in Source 73? Explain exactly what Richard Lewis is claiming in Source 76.

Case Study 2:
The Rebecca Riots

1. Introduction

The map below shows the main towns and some of the villages of West Wales in the 1830s and the major roads which joined them together:

Source 80

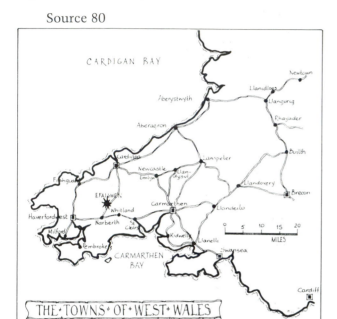

Source: P. Molloy, *And They Blessed Rebecca*, 1984.

On the map you can see marked the village of Efailwen which was on the border between the counties of Pembrokeshire and Cardiganshire. In that village on the night of 13 May 1839, a crowd of people gathered. They assembled at a gate where travellers who passed along the road which went through the village joining Narberth to Cardigan, had to stop to pay a toll for using the road. If you have ever travelled across the Severn Bridge you will know what a toll is. Perhaps some of you have also crossed the few toll bridges which we still have in Wales today. The crowd at Efailwen in May 1839 were not gathering to pay a toll, however. Armed with axes and sticks they destroyed the gate and the building (the toll house) where the tolls were collected. Once their work was completed the crowd dispersed and disappeared into the night as they had come. Within a matter of days the company which owned this road (the Whitland Turnpike Trust) had rebuilt their tollgate and tollhouse. The local magistrates had sworn people in as Special Constables to guard the gate so that it should

not be attacked again. However, on the night of 6 June 1839 a crowd gathered at the same spot, and having driven away the Special Constables, destroyed the gate and the tollhouse for a second time. When, soon afterwards, a similar attack took place in the nearby village of Maesgwyn, the magistrates became so alarmed that they asked for soldiers to be brought into the area. A small force of troops was sent and a number of individuals were arrested and accused of taking part in the attacks. The gate at Efailwen was now again rebuilt but on 17 July 1839, this time in daylight, a crowd assembled and for a third time the gate and the tollhouse were demolished. The photograph below shows the scene being re-enacted in 1964 by modern day villagers in Efailwen:

Source 81

Source: Ken Davies (Photos), Carmarthen.

What is peculiar about the person striking the gate and the persons behind him? When the third attack on the Efailwen gate took place it was reported that the leader of the crowd was a man dressed in women's clothing! He was called 'Rebecca' by his followers who were also men dressed as women, and he addressed them as his 'daughters'!

This strange occurrence was probably thought of at the time as just some odd event taking place in the 'wilds' of West Wales where many old and secret customs survived. The Whitland Turnpike Trust finally gave up trying to have a tollgate at Efailwen and the attacks therefore came to an end. For the next three and a half years nothing more was seen of the mysterious 'Rebecca' and her followers. However, just, as the incidents of 1839 were probably fading from people's memories, in October 1842, further attacks on tollgates took place at the village of St. Clears in Carmarthenshire and again these attacks were carried out by men dressed in women's clothing with a leader called 'Rebecca' at their head. In the year that followed the 'Rebecca Riots' spread to many parts of West and Mid Wales, the number of people who became involved also multiplied and the violence used by the rioters and the targets of their violence also grew. At times it must have seemed as if the whole population of West Wales was in revolt. Certainly the Government was alarmed enough to send down to West Wales a large number of soldiers to put down the riots and to set up an Enquiry to find out what the causes of these serious outbreaks were. Eventually the Government acted to reform the Turnpike Trusts but by then it was clear to the authorities that objections to the Trusts were only part of the reasons for this discontent and protest in West Wales. By 1844 with the riots coming to an end and the Turnpike Trusts being reformed, both 'Rebecca' and the Government could feel satisfied at their work. Although Rebecca did not re-appear in West Wales, her activities in the years 1839 and 1842-43, attracted a great deal of attention at the time and have gone down as one of the most important events in nineteenth-century Welsh history.

This case-study of the Rebecca Riots, looks at the *causes*, the *events* and the *results* of the movement. Section 2 will look closely at the background causes by studying the society in which they took place—the rural society of West Wales—and the immediate issue, the Turnpike Trusts, which led to their outbreak. Section 3 will look at the Riots themselves and the different phases they passed through. The Conclusion to the case-study will consider the outcome of the Riots.

2. The Background to Rebecca

THE RURAL SOCIETY OF WEST WALES

Population

The map (Source 82) shows the counties of Wales in the nineteenth century and the population figures for each of these counties in 1801 (top) and 1841 (bottom). When we refer to 'West Wales' we usually mean large parts of the former counties of Carmarthenshire, Pembrokeshire and Cardiganshire. Work out roughly what proportion of the population of Wales lived in these three counties combined in 1841.

Occupations

At the time of the Rebecca Riots the majority of people in the three counties of west Wales earned their living on the land, but there were also some industries in the area. There was a long history of coalmining in Pembrokeshire, which once had been the most important coal-mining area in Wales, but by the nineteenth century the industry was declining there. In the eastern part of Carmarthenshire the mining of coal was increasing in the early nineteenth century, but not as fast as in Glamorgan and

Source 82

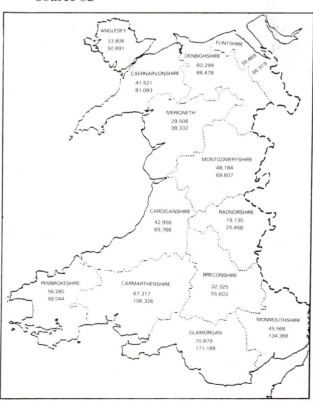

Source: Based on Census Returns 1801 and 1841.

Monmouthshire. This was because in west Wales the coal was of the anthracite type and there was not such a great demand for this. There were also ironworks and tinplate works in Carmarthenshire and at Llanelli there was copper-smelting. Cardiganshire had once had a thriving lead-mining industry, but it was declining by the early nineteenth century. The chart below shows the main occupations in west Wales in 1841 and the number of adult men employed:

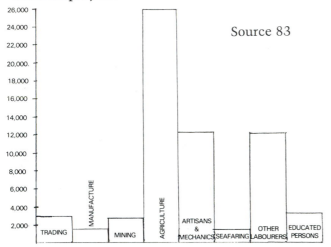

Source 83

Source: Numbers and Employment of Able-bodied adults over 21 years of age in Carmarthenshire, Cardiganshire and Pembrokeshire, 1841.

Source: Based on 1841 Census of Population.

Agriculture

Farming in west Wales in the early nineteenth century was a combination of *arable* (crop-growing) and *pastoral* (animal rearing) farming. In some areas animal rearing was more important and in others, mainly crops were grown. In the main a mixture of both was followed by farmers. How might the geography of west Wales have influenced this? The main animals raised were sheep and cattle; in some areas of west Wales 'new' crops such as potatoes and turnips were grown, but the most important crops were the ones which had been grown for centuries—barley and oats. Accounts of farming in west Wales written in the early nineteenth century point out how primitive the methods of agriculture were. Here is one such account by a visitor to the area in 1804—it is quite a difficult source and will need to be read carefully, but it does give a good impression of the nature of farming in the area:

Source 84

The ploughs of the country are . . . awkward . . . The furrow (trench) is seldom more than half turned, by which the growth of weeds is encouraged . . . Wheat is little raised, and other crops succeed each other, till nature wearied with the burden, refuses to bear it any longer . . . The land . . . is thus reduced to the last stage of poverty . . . Marl (clay used as a fertilizer), so successfully used by the English farmer, is sparingly adopted by the Welsh . . . there is a general want (lack) of draining . . . The carriages are generally drays (carts pulled by horses), or carts, waggons being seldom seen . . . In cutting wheat they still use the common reaping hook, so inferior to the sickle, but barley and oats they mow with a scythe . . .

Source: Rev. J. Evans, *Letters Written During A Tour Through South Wales,* 1804.

In parts of England, in the late 18th century and early 19th century, improvements were made in farming methods, which historians call the 'agricultural revolution'. Does Source 84 give the impression that these have spread to Wales? What particular aspects of farming in west Wales does the Reverend Evans criticise? One thing is certainly the lack of fertilizer which was being used. In fact there was some improvement in this respect as the nineteenth century wore on. This was because the fertilizer *lime*, which reduces the amount of acid in the soil, began to be used. There were plentiful supplies of lime in west Wales which could be obtained from lime quarries on the edge of the south Wales coal-field. After being quarried the lime would be burnt in kilns to reduce it to a powder and sold to farmers. Many farmers in west Wales lived a good distance away from these kilns and one problem they faced in getting lime was that they had to bring it long distances along very poor roads. We shall return later to this problem for it was to play an important part in the Rebecca Riots.

Freeholders and Leaseholders

The great majority of farmers in West Wales worked small farms. Some of these 'small farmers' actually owned the land they farmed on—they were known as 'freeholders'. However, because their farms were small these freeholders were frequently little better off financially than the labourers who worked for them. This was also true of the large number of farmers who did not own their land at all—the 'leaseholders'. They rented or 'leased' the farms they worked, from landowners. For many centuries these leases had been granted by the landowner to his tenants for very long periods—sometimes for as long as three lifetimes.

However, by the nineteenth century, new leases were granted for a limited number of years and even for one year at a time. What advantage might this have had for landowners? What disadvantages would it have had for leaseholders? How might it have had an effect on farming methods?

Landlords

Leasing arrangements also had an effect on the relations between landlords and their tenants. What might these have been? The landlords or landowners of West Wales dominated the life of West Wales, for their ownership of land gave them not just economic power but social status and political power as well. The most import-ant of the Landlords were the *gentry*—families who because of their importance, wealth and services to the Crown, had been awarded titles. In Carmarthenshire the Rice Family of *Dynevor* (their estate of 7,000 acres) and the Cawdor Family of *Golden Grove* and *Stackpole* (they had huge estates of 70,000 acres), were the most important of the gentry. In Pembroke-shire, the great families were the Philipps of *Picton Castle* and the Owens of *Orielton*. In Cardiganshire the Pryses of *Gogerddan* and the Vaughans of *Crosswood* were the important gentry. There were also the 'lesser gentry'—a large number of families who might not have a title but who sometimes owned even more land than the important gentry. Two members of the 'lesser gentry' who feature in the story of the Rebecca Riots, were William Chambers of Llanelli and Edward Crompton Lloyd-Hall of Cilgwyn.

The engraving below of Dynevor Castle where the Rice family lived, suggests the wealth and rich lifestyle of the Gentry:

Source 85

Source: Dynevor Castle in 1822. Engraving by C. Ashey, National Library of Wales.

Many of the gentry preferred to live in London or in the south of England rather than on their estates in west Wales. Why might this have been? How common this 'absenteeism' was and the effect it had, was commented upon by a visitor to Cardiganshire in 1803 as follows:

> Source 86
>
> A person . . . enumerated (counted) to me a list of properties (landowners) . . . who draw out of the county twenty-five thousand pounds annually, without ever seeing the spot from whence they derive (get) their wealth . . . this great sum is taken away . . . not by one overgrown Lord . . . but by several landowners of from one to five thousand pounds a year . . .
>
> *Source:* Benjamin Heath Malkin. *The Scenery, Antiquities and Biography of South Wales*, 1807.

The absenteeism of landlords obviously made them even more distant from their tenants than was already the case because of their wealth and lifestyle. There were also other differences between landlords and tenants. The landlords mainly spoke English and were members of the Church of England: their tenants spoke Welsh and most of them belonged to the Nonconformist churches. What effect might such differences have had on relations between the gentry and their tenants?

Political Power

Not all the members of the gentry were wealthy. Many of them—particularly those of the 'lesser gentry' who owned small estates—were heavily in debt. Partly, this was because of the lifestyle they led but it was also because of the primitive condition of farming on their estates. They all, however, had 'social posit-ion' and they also held political power in west Wales. The important gentry families domi-nated Parliamentary politics—George Trevor Rice of Dynevor became M.P. for Carmarthen-shire in 1820, Sir John Owen of Orielton was M.P. for Pembrokeshire and Richard Philipps of Picton Castle sat in the House of Commons for Haverfordwest. There was great rivalry between the gentry families to hold these positions and they were quite prepared to bribe or threaten voters to support them. As we saw in our study of the Merthyr Riots of 1831 ordinary people generally did not have the right to vote in elections at this time.

In local politics the control of the gentry was even more complete. Justices of the Peace were mainly appointed from the ranks of the lesser gentry. J.P.s had important responsibilities for law and order, and they were also the people who controlled local government. Thus they decided how money, collected through the rates, was to be spent on such things as roads and bridges and, up to 1834, the way in which relief was given to poor people. Most magistrates in west Wales, however, did very little of this work. They were quite happy to accept the title but not prepared to give up time to carry out the duties. Some of the gentry who were active J.P.s were corrupt and used their power for their own interest. How might they do this? Why would so many of the gentry want to be magistrates if they were not keen to do this work?

The Life of the Ordinary People

The farmers and labourers who made up the vast majority of the population of west Wales lived a very different kind of life from the gentry. During the course of the Rebecca Riots a journalist called Thomas Campbell Foster, who worked for the famous newspaper *The Times*, was sent down to west Wales from London to report on what was happening. His reports tell us a great deal about west Wales at this time. Here is a report on the type of housing which Foster found farm labourers living in and it is followed by a photograph of a typical farmer's cottage in Cardiganshire:

Source 87

I entered several farm labourers' cottages by the roadside . . . and found them mud hovels, the floors of mud and full of holes, without chairs or tables, generally half filled with peat packed up in every corner. Beds there were none; nothing but loose straw and filthy rags upon them. Peat fires on the floors in a corner filling the cottages with smoke, and three or four children huddled around them. In the most miserable part of St. Giles (a slum area of London), in no part of England, did I ever witness such abject poverty.

Source: The Times, 7 October, 1843.

Source 88

Source: Cardiganshire Cottage in the Nineteenth Century. National Museum of Wales.

Foster also supplies the following information on the diet of small farmers and their families:

Source 89

The small farmer here breakfasts on oatmeal and water boiled called 'duffey' or 'flummery' or on a few mashed potatoes . . . He dines on potatoes and buttermilk, with sometimes a little white Welsh cheese and barley bread, and as an occasional treat he has a salt herring. Fresh meat is never seen on the Farmer's table. He sups (has supper) on mashed potatoes. His butter he never tastes . . . beef or mutton . . . never form the farmer's food . . . Labourers . . . live entirely on potatoes, and have seldom enough of them, having only one meal a day . . .
Source: The Times, 2 December, 1843.

Why was Foster particularly surprised by the fact that farmers never ate meat or butter? Why do you think these things were not eaten? Although Foster notes here that labourers had an even worse diet than farmers, he also pointed out in other reports that there was far less difference in lifestyle between farmers and labourers in West Wales compared to what he had seen in England. For example they both worked the same long hours (up to 16 hours a day at busy times of the year) and shared back-breaking work in the fields.

The great poverty of the people was made worse quite often by the harsh attitude of their landlords. As well as paying the rent for their land and sometimes having to do other services for the landlord (such as grinding his corn) they might also have to pay *tithes* to him. Tithes were a tenth of everyone's produce which originally had to be paid annually to the local Church, but by the nineteenth century many landowners had bought the right to receive tithes and after the Tithe Commutation Act of 1836 these had to be paid in money. The attitude of landowners and the poverty of the farmers can be seen below in the evidence given by a farmer's wife to the Government Enquiry into the Rebecca Riots in 1844:

Source 90

. . . Last time when I had the tithe to pay, I could only make up seven sovereigns . . . he (the landlord's agent) refused to take them and trust me for a week or two for the rest, till I could sell something . . . I have nursed sixteen children and never owed a farthing . . . but we are worse off . . . than ever. Yet my husband has not spent sixpence in beer these twenty years . . . nor can I or the children go to church or chapel for want of decent clothing. We perhaps might have gone on but now this tithe comes so heavy . . .
Source: Evidence of Mary Thomas of Llanelli to *Commission of Inquiry Into South Wales*, 1844.

It would seem that when Mary Thomas talks here of 'going on' she means that her husband would have to apply to the authorities for help because of their great poverty. The *Poor Law* allowed magistrates to use part of the rates for 'relief' of poverty. Up to 1834 this relief would be given in the form of money or food, but after the *Poor Law Amendment Act* of that year relief could only be received by entering a workhouse where one existed.

Reading the description below by Thomas Campbell Foster of a Workhouse in West Wales will perhaps help to understand why many farmers and labourers preferred to nearly starve rather than enter a workhouse. This description is followed by a photograph of the stone-breaking cells at Cardigan Workhouse—inmates in the workhouse would be locked inside with an amount of stones which they had to break and then pass through the grill at the side of the doors. What would be the point of making them do such work?

Source 91

Agricultural labourers . . . arrive at actually the starvation point . . . rather than apply for poor relief, knowing that if they do so they will be dragged into the Union Workhouse, where they will be placed themselves in one yard, their wives in another, their male children in a third and their daughters in a fourth . . . The bread which I saw in a Workhouse is made entirely of barley and is nearly black. It has a gritty and rather sour taste . . .
Source: The Times, 27 June, 1843.

Source 92

Source: P. Molloy, *And They Blessed Rebecca*, 1984.

More workhouses were being built in west Wales in the early 1840s because poverty was increasing rapidly. This was partly due to the increase in population that was taking place. Source 82 shows that this was happening all over Wales (as it was in the rest of Britain). The rise in population was taking place in the three west Wales counties despite the fact that thousands of people were leaving the area to find work in the iron and coal industries in south Wales. This increase in the number of people meant that despite the spread of *enclosures* (which increased the amount of land used for farming) there was still not enough land available for all those people who wanted to become farmers. Even when some larger farms were broken up into smaller units the farms which resulted were often too small for a farmer to make a living from them. Landlords were able to take advantage of this 'land hunger' by charging higher rents when they leased out land. Even those people who gave up trying to have a farm of their own and worked as agricultural labourers found work very hard to find and when they did so they found wages were falling because of the abundance of labour.

Adding to this poverty was the general depression in agriculture at this time, which was particularly bad during the period of the Rebecca Riots. This depression resulted from a fall in demand for agricultural produce and the falling prices of such produce. Here a corn dealer from St. Clears giving evidence to the Government Commissioners enquiring into the causes of the Rebecca Riots, further explains what caused this depression and what its effects were:

> Source 93
>
> In the year 1840, which was a very wet summer, nearly all the farmers . . . had to purchase corn, either for seed or bread . . . This distress has not been the result of one, two or three years, but a series of at least twenty . . . The capital (value of his land and property) of the farmer for the last few years has diminished (decreased) in value, while the rates, taxes, tithes . . . and rent have been increased.
>
> *Source:* Evidence of James Rogers to *Commission of Inquiry Into South Wales,* 1844.

Protest and Public Opinion

It will be useful at this stage to try and summarize the evidence presented on the causes of the Rebecca Riots by looking at a Source which attempts to do this. Below is part of a letter left at the office of a newspaper in Carmarthen in 1843. The letter was left anonymously and was signed by 'Rebecca'! The purpose of the letter was to point out the distress and discontent in west Wales which had led to the appearance of Rebecca:

> Source 94
>
> The people, the masses to a man throughout the three counties of Carmarthen, Cardigan, and Pembroke are with me. Oh yes, they are all my children. When I meet the lime-men on the road covered with sweat and dust, I know they are Rebeccaites. When I see the coalmen coming to town clothed in rags, hard worked and hard fed, I know they are mine, they are Rebecca's children. When I see the farmers' wives carrying loaded baskets to market, bending under the weight, I know well that these are my daughters. If I turn into a farmer's house and see them eating barley bread and drinking whey (watery milk), surely, say I, these are members of my family, these are the oppressed sons and daughters of Rebecca.
>
> *Source: The Welshman,* 1 September 1843.

The point could be made that many of the things mentioned in this letter had existed in west Wales for a long time before the Rebecca Riots broke out. Why was it not until 1839 that such a protest took place? Two things can be said in answer to this. In the first place there *had* been protest before in west Wales; secondly, there were 'new' factors which did lead to the Rebecca Riots taking place when they did.

Violent protests had taken place in the town of Carmarthen in 1801 and 1818 when riots had taken place due to the shortage and high price of food and again in 1831 during the 'Reform Crisis' (dealt with in the first case-study in this book). In 1831 Carmarthen, with a population of 10,000 (compared with Cardiff with 6,000) was a large town by the standards of the time and had grown in importance as a market town and a port. There was a great deal of poverty in the town and this played an important part in the riots.

In the countryside of west Wales throughout the late 18th century and early 19th century there was also a great deal of unrest. There were frequent disturbances and crimes such as sheepstealing. Much of this was probably ordinary crime, but on some occasions it seems to have been much more a form of protest against poverty and the harshness of landlords.

For example, in 1815 and 1816 crowds of farmers in Cardiganshire attacked officials who were surveying land (land which up to then had been for everyone's use) ready for it to be enclosed and bought by landowners. Threatening letters were often sent to landlords and sometimes were followed by attacks on their property. There was also the tradition of what was known as the *ceffyl pren* (wooden horse) in which it is possible to see the roots of the Rebecca Riots. *Ceffyl pren* involved carrying a person, who was unpopular for some reason in the community, on a wooden pole or ladder. Sometimes it was an effigy of a person rather than the person. The idea was to make them look silly and to show them how badly they were thought of in the community. A kind of pantomime or mock trial was often held as well and the event usually took place at night; sometimes men dressed in women's clothing. Often the person being mocked had committed what the community thought was a moral crime (such as adultery), but at other times the person carried on the *ceffyl pren* had shown some favour to a landlord or agreed to some demand by a landlord which the farmers had resisted. Either way this was a form of protest. It was also a rejection of the existing law of the magistrates for the people's own law. Here is a report on *Ceffyl Pren* incidents in Cardiganshire in 1839.

Source 95

At the present time the magistrates of Cardigan and its vicinity are greatly embarrassed by the increasing practice, called the Ceffyl Pren or wooden horse; a figure of a horse is carried at night in the midst of a mob with their faces blackened, and torches in their hands, to the door of any person whose conduct may have exposed him to the censure (disapproval) of his neighbours, or who may have rendered (made) himself unpopular, by informing against another, and by contributing to enforce (carry out) the law.

Source: Report on the Constabulary Force of England and Wales, 1839.

It is also important to remember that there was no proper police force in the West Wales counties to deal with incidents such as the *Ceffyl Pren* and the Rebecca Riots when they broke out. An Act of Parliament passed in 1839 allowed counties to set up police forces, but the expense involved decided the magistrates of West Wales against it. They still hoped that swearing-in Special Constables would be sufficient to deal with any trouble which would arise. If not, local Yeomanry and soldiers would have to be sent for.

The 'new factors' which played a part in the background to the Rebecca Riots were to do with the growth of public opinion which criticised the state of things in West Wales and the role of the gentry.

In the early nineteenth century the first popular newspapers were set up in West Wales —*The Carmarthen Journal* (a Conservative paper), *The Welshman* (which was Radical in Politics) and *The Cambrian*. *The Welshman* in particular attacked the poverty and bad social conditions which existed in the area and encouraged the farmers to protest and take action about them. One of its main targets was the new Poor Law of 1834, which both increased the rates and created the workhouses with their harsh treatment of the poor. A Carmarthen lawyer, Hugh Williams, was particularly active in this campaign. Williams (shown in the Source below) was a Radical who in 1838 helped to set up the first Chartist 'branch' in Wales at Carmarthen. Chartism (a movement which campaigned for greater political power for working people) will be looked at in the next case-study in this book. Although Chartist ideas spread throughout west Wales, observers such as Thomas Campbell Foster of *The Times* believed that they did not have much influence on the farmers of the area. However, Hugh Williams does seem to have been an influential figure, and at one time it was even thought that he was 'Rebecca':

Source 96

Source: Portrait of Hugh Williams, National Library of Wales.

Source 107

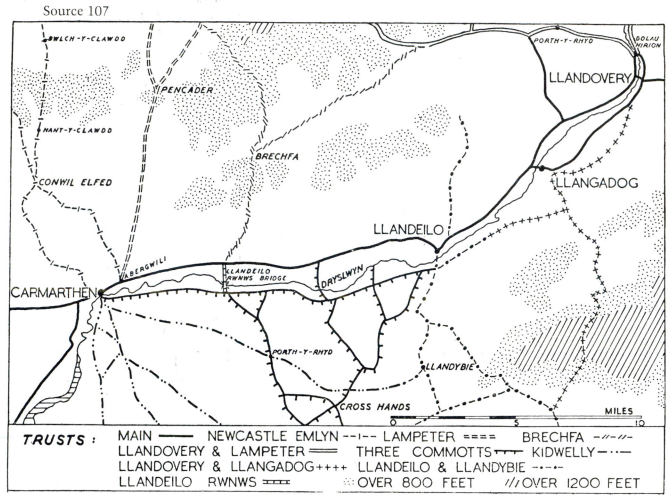

Source: Turnpike Trusts in the Towy Valley, Carmarthenshire. David Williams, *The Rebecca Riots*, 1955.

3. The Riots

THE ARRIVAL OF REBECCA

Efailwen 1839

The winter of 1838-39 was a particularly hard one in West Wales and the poor harvest which followed in 1839 brought great suffering and poverty to the farmers of West Wales. In many parts of the three counties in the early months of 1839 there were localized protests against burdens upon the farmers such as tithes and the Poor Law and many incidents in which the *ceffyl pren* was used were reported. In Pembrokeshire the Whitland Turnpike Trust at the end of 1838 had placed its toll-collecting in the hands of Thomas Bullin. One of the changes he made to the Trust's operations was to put up more tollgates and to increase toll charges. Four new gates were placed near to the village of Efailwen and this seems to have been

the final straw for the hard-pressed farmers of this area and it was here that Rebecca and her supporters first appeared on the night of 13 May 1839 to attack the new gates and the tollhouse. The print (Source 109) shows a visit by the Rebecca rioters to a tollgate—who is the person on horseback meant to be?

Immediately, there was a great deal of interest and speculation as to who 'Rebecca' really was. As has been mentioned earlier, people thought it was the Carmarthen Chartist, Hugh Williams. Levi Gibbon, a farmer who took part in the first Rebecca incidents at Efailwen, however, suggested that Rebecca was in fact Thomas Rees, a small farmer from the parish of Mynachlog-ddu. There follows part of a poem written by Levi Gibbon in which he points to this identification and a photograph of Thomas Rees' farm, Carnabwth.

Source 109

Source: The Rebecca Rioters. The *Illustrated London News.*

Source 110

Rebecca, like myself was born in Wales
In the parish of Mynachlog Ddu—a bonny child
She grew up to be quite tall
And she took possession of the gate at Efailwen.

Source 111

Source: Thomas Rees' Farm, Carnabwth. P. Molloy. *And They Blessed Rebecca*, 1984.

If it was Thomas Rees at Efailwen in May 1839 it certainly was *not* him later on, for we know that he took no further part in the Rebecca Riots. In any event by the late summer of 1839 the events at Efailwen had passed and Rebecca (whoever she was) and her followers had seemingly disappeared. There were to be no further disturbances at Efailwen after July 1839 and if it was not for the re-appearance of Rebecca over three years later, the events which had taken place there might long ago have been forgotten.

Rebecca Re-appears 1842

The early 1840s saw a continuing pattern of hard winters followed by poor harvests and great poverty in West Wales. Even when there was a good harvest in 1842 the depression in the area did not come to an end, for in the same year there was industrial unrest in South Wales which led to a fall in demand for the farm produce of the three western counties. In October 1842 the Main Turnpike Trust decided to open a number of new gates on its roads to stop people who had been avoiding paying tolls. The map (Source 112) shows some of the roads of the Main and other Turnpike Trusts on the Carmarthenshire—Pembrokeshire border.

On the night of 18 November 1842 Rebecca and her followers suddenly re-appeared to destroy tollgates at Pwll-Trap and Mermaid, near the town of St. Clears in Carmarthenshire.

It was in July 1843 that the first Rebecca-type incidents took place in this area. One of these was at Llangyfelach near Swansea. After an attack there the Chief Constable of Glamorgan (a county which did have a small police force, unlike the three west Wales counties), Captain Charles Napier, tried to arrest a man who had been informed upon, for his part in the attack. In the process of doing this Napier was himself violently attacked. On 2 August 1843 the first Rebecca attack at Llanelli took place when the tollgate at Sandy Gate was destroyed. Here is part of the evidence given to the magistrates by the tollgate-keeper and his wife as to what happened on that night.

> Source 134
>
> He told his wife that he was afraid that the gate would be broken that night . . . He had received several joking letters about the gate . . . At about one o'clock in the morning he heard people striking at the iron posts of the gate. He looked out the window and saw people sawing the tollgate. Immediately after, two shots were fired through the window. Two or three people who had their faces blacked broke the door in. He then went out . . . and went on his knees begging them not to take the house down upon his children, and to let him get his wife, children, and furniture out . . . They said "Take it down, don't stop, take it down, to the devil with them" . . . Somebody fired a shot into the house . . . The people then went away . . . The windows were broken in and the porch . . . broken down. They pulled down the dresser and also the mantelpiece.
>
> *Source:* Evidence of Jenkin Hugh of Llanelli and Catherine Hugh, taken on oath 14 August, 1843, before Magistrates. National Library of Wales.

Source 135 shows another contemporary print of Rebeccaites.

Compare this illustration (Source 135) with earlier illustrations you have seen (Sources 109 and 114). What difference is there? Three men were arrested for the attack described in Source 134—two of them were labourers but none of them were farmers. Compare the description of this attack with earlier ones. Having done all this and thought about it, what might have been the other fear of the 'respectable farmers' of West Wales which turned them away from the Rebecca attacks?

Dai'r Cantwr and Shoni Sgubor Fawr

Two men were known to be particularly active in the riots in this new area of Rebecca activity—John Jones and David Davies of Pontyberem

Source 135

Source: Rebeccaites. The *Illustrated London News.*

in Carmarthenshire. John Jones was better known by his Welsh nickname of *Shoni Sgubor Fawr* which came from a farm that he had worked at in Penderyn, Glamorgan, near to Merthyr Tydfil where he was born. Shoni had later left his work as an agricultural labourer to become a soldier, but after leaving the army he became better known as a heavy drinker and prize-fighter in Merthyr where he was often arrested for his wild behaviour. At the time of the Rebecca Riots of 1843 Shoni was 32 years old and by then he had lived in Pontyberem for a number of years and had been employed as a copper-worker and a labourer. It was in Pontyberem that he formed his friendship with David Davies, a coalminer. Davies was also better known by his Welsh nickname which he earned because he wrote poetry—*Dai'r Cantwr*. Like Shoni he came originally from Glamorgan, having been born at Llancarfan in the Vale of Glamorgan. He too had started his working life as a farm labourer but had moved around South Wales working as a quarryman and an ironworker before coming to Pontyberem in 1843 when he was 30 years old. Unlike Shoni, Dai did not have a background of being a wild and violent man. In fact he was well known as a lay-preacher in Wesleyan Chapels. We shall return shortly to Shoni and Dai, but neither of them was present at Pontarddulais in September 1843 when one of the most serious of all the Rebecca disturbances took place, and it is that which we will consider now.

The Pontarddulais Attack

At midnight on the 6 September, 1843 at Pontarddulais a crowd of over a hundred Rebeccaites appeared and began to attack a tollgate in the village. Someone, however, had tipped off the authorities about the attack and a force of soldiers and police led by Chief Constable Napier lay in wait. Once the attack on the gate began Napier appeared to challenge the crowd and shots were fired at him. A local magistrate, William Chambers, relates below what then happened:

Source 136

The firing continued from 7 to 10 minutes, during which 60 or 70 shots were fired . . . He saw William Hugh getting from the road over the Gate of the field in which the soldiers were, upon which the soldiers followed him . . . He was caught at the bottom of the hill . . . He was dressed as he then was, in girl's clothes and had his face blackened . . . On getting up to Pontardulais Gate . . . he found the gate entirely destroyed and the windows of the Toll house and the whole of the inside of it destroyed, and three men lying hand cuffed on the floor . . .

Source: Evidence of William Chambers to Magistrates, 8 September, 1843. National Library of Wales.

In fact seven people were arrested for their part in this attack and on 26 October 1843 they were brought to trial at Cardiff Assizes. John Hughes, one of the leaders of the attack, was sentenced to 20 years transportation and John Hugh and David Jones to seven years transportation each. Here is part of the speech made by the trial Judge before he sentenced these men and this is followed by a public confession which the three men issued after the trial. Why would this confession be issued like this?

Source 137

John Hughes, David Jones and John Hugh. You stand convicted of a felony (a serious crime) . . . Until of late such crimes were of very, very unfrequent occurrence (didn't often happen) in this country. The interruption (sentence) you receive will, perhaps, prevent the repetition of the crime . . . John Hughes, your conduct at the times, as well as the papers found in your pocket, demonstrated that you were a leader . . . mercy cannot be expected if offences of this kind are repeated and the peace of the country is not fully restored . . .

Source: Quoted in P. Molloy, *And They Blessed Rebecca*, 1984.

Source 138

A LETTER.

"To the Public generally, and to our Neighbours in particular.

"WE, John Hughes, David Jones, and John Hugh, now lying in Cardiff gaol, convicted of the attack on Pontarddulais turnpike gate, and the police stationed there to protect it—being now sentenced to transportation, beg, and earnestly call on others to take warning by our fate, and to stop in their mad course, before they fall into our condemnation.

"We are guilty, and doomed to suffer, while hundreds have escaped. Let them, and every one, take care not to be deluded again to attack public or private property, and resist the power of the law, for it will overtake them with vengeance, and bring them down to destruction.

"We are only in prison now, but in a week or two shall be banished as rogues—to be slaves to strangers, in a strange land. We must go, in the prime of life, from our dear homes, to live and labour with the worst of villains—looked upon as thieves.

"Friends—neighbours—all—but especially young men—keep from night meetings! Fear to do wrong, and dread the terrors of the judge.

"Think of what we must, and you may suffer, before you dare to do as we have done.

"If you will be peaceable, and live again like honest men, by the blessing of God, you may expect to prosper; and we, poor outcast wretches, may have to thank you for the mercy of the Crown—for on no other terms than your good conduct will any pity be shewn to us, or others, who may fall into our almost hopeless situation.

(Signed)

"JOHN HUGHES,
"DAVID JONES,
"The ✗ mark of JOHN HUGH.

"Cardiff Gaol. Nov. 1st, 1843.

"Witness, JOHN B. WOODS, Governor."

Source: Confession of John Hughes, David Jones, John Hugh. National Library of Wales.

Rioting Continues

Obviously the authorities had hoped that the arrests at Pontarddulais and the sentences handed-out at the trial would see an end to the riots in South-East Carmarthenshire and Glamorgan. However, as Thomas Campbell Foster points out below, this was not to be:

Source 139

It was fondly hoped and indeed confidently predicted by both the magistrates and the police that it would put an end to Rebeccaism and that such would be the terror felt throughout the country that the Lady Rebecca would be so struck with terror that the outrages would at once be put an end to. The effect has, however, been precisely the reverse. The Welsh are a peculiar people and they have become completely exasperated (irritated) in consequence (because of) of their countrymen having been shot, as they say, by a villainous body of police.

Source: The Times, 20 September, 1843.

Within two days of the Pontarddulais attack, another serious Rebecca incident took place at Hendy tollhouse. During the destruction of the gate and tollhouse there, the tollkeeper, a 75 year old woman called Sarah Davies, was killed. Dai'r Cantwr and Shoni Sgubor Fawr were probably involved in this attack and during the rest of September they and their followers terrorized the area to the north-west of Llanelli. Here is evidence on some of their activities later given to the Magistrates by informers:

Source 140

About 9 o'clock . . . he heard a man calling him out of bed, and Shoni Sgubor Fawr came into the room . . . he had a single barrelled gun in his hand. From fear he went with him . . . and they went together to the mountain and there they met another party headed by Dai y Cantwr . . . in a shawl and bonnet. They proceeded towards Pontyberem and went to Mr. New-man's house, (the owner of Pontyberem Iron-works) where they made a great noise and fired several shots . . . Shoni said that Slocombe (a clerk in the employ of Mr. Newman) must leave in a week, for no Englishman should manage in Wales any more. If he did not he would be killed and his house pulled down . . .

Source: Evidence of David Lewis of Trimsaran to Magistrates, 26 September,1843. National Library of Wales.

Source 141

. . . I was called upon by Shoni Sgubor Fawr and went with the party. On my way I had a conver-sation with Dai'r Cantwr . . . I was coming up Gellygwlwnog field arm in arm with him after burning Mr. Chambers's (a local landowner and Magistrate) Ricks of hay . . . I asked him how they got the Ricks to take fire. He said that 3 or 4 had matches under the Ricks lighted and the rest with Guns watching . . .

Source: Evidence of Thomas Phillips of Topsail to Magistrates, 12 December, 1843. National Library of Wales.

As Thomas Campbell Foster points out below the activities of Dai and Shoni and the violence used now began to turn away many people who had once supported Rebecca:

Source 142

It is said that the better class of farmers are beginning to sicken of Rebecca's proceedings, and with some reason. I am informed that a kind of blackmail is levied upon them . . . Money is raised by sending round notices to farmers to pay certain sums at certain times . . . if they refuse, they do it at the peril of having their stacks fired. This . . . has caused a great deal of secret information to be given by them to the authorities . . .

Source: The Times, 25 September, 1843.

In addition to this the Government were now urging the authorities in West Wales to take more action against the remaining Rebeccaites. 150 more Metropolitan policemen and addit-ional marines were brought into the area and more farmers were now prepared to serve as special constables. As the poster (Source 143) shows large sums of money were offered to those who were prepared to inform on the Rebeccaites.

Source 143

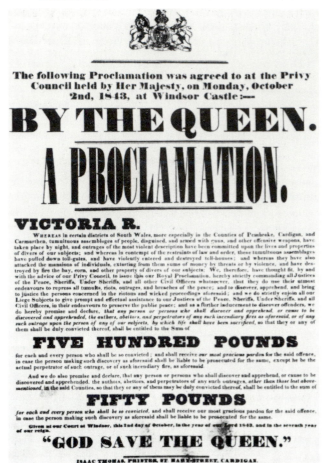

Source: Reward Poster, October 1843. National Library of Wales.

These various efforts by the authorities had an effect, for the attack carried out on 23 Sept-ember 1843 (described in Source 140) was to be Dai and Shoni's last. Soon after, they were informed upon and arrested. On 27 December 1843 they and thirty-nine of their followers were placed on trial at Carmarthen Assizes. They were found guilty of the charges brought against them and this is what the trial Judge had to say in sentencing them:

Source 144

Probably the greater portion of your life will be spent in a foreign land and how different will be your position then to what it is here. You will be compelled to work but will receive no payment for your labours except such food as will serve to support you . . . You will not be in name, but in reality, slaves. To that I must sentence you. The sentence of the court is that you John Jones will be transported beyond the seas for the term of your natural life, and that you David Davies be transported for twenty years.

Source: The Welshman, 5 January, 1844.

Both men laughed as they left the dock but within days their defiance broke—they confessed their crimes and informed on others. Before leaving for a convict colony in Australia, Dai'r Cantwr, the poet, composed the following verses. What attitude does he show here?

Source 145

Though wounding were the wicked blows
The cruel world hath struck at me
I have a strength they cannot break
My human pride my dignity
They bound my hands with prison chains
And yet my soul they could not bind
Now far across the sundering sea
I drag my sorely troubled mind
My father's home its tender care
I know I shall not even see again
I'll rot for twenty searing years
Among corrupt unfeeling men
Farewell to you a hundredfold
Fair country, sweet untroubled Wales
Still I remember in my pain
Your streams your hills your gentle vales
You are the garden of the world
The Eden where all beauty lies
My heart breaks as with flaming sword
They drive me now from paradise.

Source: Dai Cantwr's Threnody.

The End of Rebecca

Even now the Rebecca movement did not die out completely, however. Isolated outbreaks took place well into 1844 in South-West Carmarthenshire and Cardiganshire, where Rebecca had first started. The Rebecca attacks even spread into areas where they had not occurred before, such as the Upper Wye Valley in Radnorshire. Landlords still received threatening letters such as this:

Source 146

"Carabunda Castle, Dec. 16, 1843
Sir/ I am given to understand that you are habit of receiving your Rents from your Tenants at Llanelly and the neighbourhood and giving them durty pint or a quart of Beeor in the shape of present. It is very improper for you to do as a Gentleman but now in future do not degrade yourself in that manner and if you do my ould Mother Rebecca will come and pay you a vicit in the corse of this spring your Caretter is so degraded you should do sumthing more hansome for to gain your caretter to its former state and if do not you will draw the indignant spirit of my old Mother Becca to save depradations behave yourself as a Man you have acted as a traitor to the working men of the Nighbourhood now Mr. Chambers for god sake do not force me to work I am one of the Daughters of Rebecca.''

Source: Letter sent to William Chambers, Llanelli. National Library of Wales.

In the 1850s, 60s and 70s there were widespread attacks by people dressed as Rebecca and her Daughters on salmon weirs in the Upper Wye Valley in Radnorshire which one historian has called 'The Second Rebecca Riots'. As will be noted in the final case-study in this book, the farmers and labourers of North-east Wales who protested about the payment of tithes in the 1880s, liked to think of themselves as the 'Rebecca of North Wales'.

However, although there continued to be widespread discontent and protest throughout rural West-Wales and other parts of Wales, after the end of 1843, this was more or less what might be regarded as the 'normal' level of disturbances. To all intents and purposes the Rebecca Riots of 1839 and 1842-43 had finally come to an end.

4. Conclusion and Aftermath

A combination of firm action and strong punishments meted out by the authorities and the way in which most of the small farmers of West Wales turned away from violent to peaceful action, helped to bring an end to the Rebecca Riots. The Government had also taken positive measures to enquire into what were the obviously deeply-felt grievances of the farmers of West Wales. After an initial brief enquiry had revealed that there were many genuine griev-

ances in October 1843 a full *Commission of Enquiry* was set up under the Chairmanship of the Landowner and public Servant, Thomas Frankland Lewis. The Commission very quickly collected evidence (some of which has been looked at here), mostly from the local gentry and Magistrates but also from some farmers. Its Report was published in March 1844 and here is how it summed up what it believed to be the causes of the Rebecca Riots:

Source 147

It appeared generally, that the chief grounds of complaint were the mismanagement of the funds applicable to turnpike roads, the frequency and the amount of the payments of tolls, and, in some cases, the conduct of toll collectors, and the illegal demands made by them: the increase in the amount payable for tithe under the Tithe Commutation Act . . . the operation of the Poor Law Amendment Act, principally (though not exclusively) on account of the high salaries of the officers, the administration of justice by the local magistrates and especially the amount of the fees paid to their clerks, and the progressive increase of the county rate . . . All persons acquainted with the condition of the country concurred in stating that a succession of wet and unproductive harvests had very much reduced the capital of the farmers. They had been forced, during successive years, to buy the bread consumed in their families; and the money they obtained by the sale of stock, and the other produce of their farms, scarcely enabled them to make good various payments to which they were liable.

Concurrently with these difficulties, the price of sheep, cattle, and butter had fallen much below the average of preceding years, though, at the same time, (as it is said) all rates, tithes, and taxes had increased, the rent of land still remaining, generally, undiminished.

Source: Report of the Commission of Inquiry into South Wales, 1844.

The Report also criticised the ignorance of the Welsh language by the magistrates which it argued did not help them to carry out their work of upholding law and order. It went no further, however, in criticising the gentry and landlords of West Wales. They also made a number of firm recommendations for reforming the Turnpike Trusts including the introduction of equal tolls and the setting up of Road Boards in each county to take control of the roads. The Government accepted these recommendations and they were made law in August 1844. As a result the Turnpike Trusts of West Wales were thoroughly reformed and for many years South Wales was to have the best road system in Britain.

Speculation continued as to who 'Rebecca' really was, but it was becoming clear that there never had been any one Rebecca, but a number who took on the role of leading the discontented of their areas in West Wales. Dai, Shoni and the 3 men transported for their part in the Pontardulais attack were certainly some of these 'Rebeccas'. John Hughes was eventually pardoned in 1857 with 6½ years of his sentence left and he decided to settle in Tasmania, Australia. He can be seen here at his farm in Australia in later years.

Source 148

Source: John Hughes in Tasmania. D. Williams, *The Rebecca Riots*, 1955.

John Hughes served out his sentence and became a free man in December 1850. David Jones was not so lucky for he died in July 1844 in Australia, only 21 years old. Both Dai and Shoni maintained their reputation for being troublesome characters in Australia and with no pardon for good behaviour they were forced to serve out their full sentences. Dai returned to Wales when his sentence was finished and fullfilled his wish to die in his beloved homeland.

By the time Dai'r Cantwr returned to Wales these men had been virtually forgotten but the grievances which led them and others like them to join in the activities of Rebecca continued. As has been seen, the abuses of the Turnpike Trusts were only a part of those grievances and so the reform of the Trusts alone did not remove them. The growth of the coal industry in South Wales and emigration to countries across the sea, did allow many people to leave West Wales and find new lives elsewhere. This helped to relieve many of the pressures of a growing population which had made poverty and distress in West Wales so bad. However, other grievances and poverty remained a part of the way of life of the area.

The question therefore might be asked as to whether the Rebecca Rioters of the late 1830s and early 1840s in West Wales were justified in their actions and if they in any way succeeded in what might have been their aims. Perhaps we might turn here to the view of Thomas Frankland Lewis who was Chairman of the Government Enquiry of 1844. Eight years afterwards he gave this view about the Rebecca Riots:

> Source 149
> The people saw that their only remedy was to take the law into their own hands. The Rebecca conspiracy was organised with much skill, and carried through with much fidelity (loyalty) . . . It was never diverted from its original purpose, and the instant that purpose seem likely to be attained, that is to say the instant that an enquiry into the Welsh turnpike system was instituted (set up) by the government, the association was dissolved and no one has ever proposed its revival. The Rebecca Riots are a very creditable portion of Welsh History.
>
> *Source:* E. Evans, 'Nassau Senior in Wales'. *National Library of Wales Journal,* 1951.

FURTHER WORK ON THE EVIDENCE

1. Look carefully at Source 84 and then attempt the questions below:
   a. What type of historical evidence do you think this is? Is it reliable evidence for the state of farming in West Wales in the early nineteenth century? Explain your answer.
   b. What is meant by the phrase 'till nature wearied with the burden, refuses to bear it any longer'?
   c. What other criticisms are made of the way agriculture is carried out in West Wales?

2. Look at Source 93 and then consider the following questions:
   a. Why do you think it is important that this man reports that farmers are buying corn for bread and seed?
   b. What does this man blame for the distress in farming in West Wales at this time?
   c. Do you think this man is in a good position to give us reliable evidence on the condition of farming in West Wales at this time? What other evidence might you look at to back up this Source? Explain your answers.

3. Look carefully at Sources 97 and 98 and then answer these questions:
   a. Why does Source 97 suggest that the Rebecca Rioters took their lead from the Bible?
   b. What do you think is meant by the word 'seed' in Source 97? Who would this be in the case of the Rebecca Rioters?
   c. What is meant in Source 98 by the phrase 'a considerable degree of religious fanaticism'?
   d. What in Source 98 backs up the view that the Rebecca Rioters took their lead from the Bible?
   e. Who was the author of Source 98? From what you have found out about him in this case-study was he in a good position to provide us with reliable evidence on the Rebecca Riots? Explain your answer.

4. Look at Source 103 and then answer the following:
   a. Try to find out what each of these were—Landau; Curricle; Gig; Wain. Explain what they were and why it is important to understand the meaning of such words when using this Source.

b. How much is charged at this Tollgate for carriages and how much for horses drawing a waggon?

c. Why do you think there is a lower toll for carriages drawn by asses than carriages drawn by horses?

d. What item in this list of charges was to play an important part in the Rebecca Riots and why?

e. Do you think this Source is reliable evidence for the charges made by Turnpike Trusts in West Wales? Explain your answer.

5. Look carefully at Source 107 and then answer the questions below:
   a. Find the villages of Pencader and Llandybie on the map. To travel from Pencader to Llandybie how many Turnpike Trust roads would have to be used. Name the roads.
   b. What would happen when someone changed from travelling on one Turnpike Trust road to another.
   c. Why did farmers from the Pencader area make regular journeys to villages in the area where Llandybie is?

6. Look at Sources 119 and 121 and then consider these questions:
   a. As historical evidence what do these two Sources have in common?
   b. What difference between them might make one of them more reliable as first-hand historical evidence? Explain your answer.
   c. What does the following phrase in Source 119 mean—'do not even get one half of what is collected for them'?
   d. What is meant by the phrase 'avoid attending nightly meetings and committing acts of outrage' in Source 121?
   e. Which of these Sources do you think is more reliable as a guide to the attitude which people held in West Wales towards the Rebecca Rioters? Explain your answer.

7. Look at Sources 129 and 130 and then consider the following questions?
   a. Who has been attacked in Source 129 and where has the attack been carried out?
   b. Who is being offered a pardon in Source 129 and why?
   c. What has been attacked in Source 130 and why would Rebecca supporters have attacked this?
   d. What threat is issued in Source 130?
   e. What does the word 'felonious' in Source 129 mean and the word 'nefarious' in Source 130? Why is it important to know the meaning of these words?

f. What does Source 130 say directly which Source 129 only suggests?

8. Having looked at Sources 109, 114 and 135 answer these questions:
   a. What is each of these illustrations meant to show?
   b. What differences are shown in the headgear worn by Rebeccaites?
   c. What is being carried by the Rebeccaites in Source 135 which is not being carried by them in Sources 109 and 114? What is the significance of this?
   d. Why did the Rebeccaites wear the kind of disguises shown in the illustrations?
   e. Before you could accept these illustrations as accurate records of what the Rebeccaites looked like, what would you need to know? Do you think these illustrations are accurate on this basis? Explain your answer.

9. Look at Source 138 and then answer the following questions:
   a. Who are the three men who have written this Source?
   b. What sentence did they receive for their attack on the Pontarddulais Gate?
   c. What do they mean when they say they are to be 'slaves to strangers, in a strange land'?
   d. Why do you think this letter was published?
   e. What doubts might you have about the reliability of this Source?

10. Look carefully at Source 147 and then answer the following questions:
    a. A number of grievances which farmers had against Turnpike Trusts are mentioned here but one of their grievances against the Trust is not mentioned. What is it? Looking back to Source 104 will help you.
    b. The payment of Tithes is also mentioned in the Source as a grievance, but precisely why the farmers objected to this is not mentioned. What was their objection and why do you think it is not mentioned here?
    c. What aspect of grievances felt by the people of West Wales against the Poor Laws is not mentioned? Source 91 will also help you here.
    d. Remembering what you saw in Part 2 of this case-study, do you think that any of the grievances of farmers which we looked at there are not mentioned in this Source. Why do you think this is?
    e. On the basis of the answers you have given to the above questions, do you think this Source is a full and reliable piece of evidence on the causes of the Rebecca Riots?

Chartism in Wales

1. Introduction: Background to Welsh Chartism

Politics in Early Nineteenth Century Wales

Politics in Wales in the first half of the nineteenth century, was dominated by the upper classes. When elections for Members of Parliament took place, very few people had the right to vote. Usually local landowners could rely on those people who did have the vote to support them, their family, or the candidates they put forward in elections. Why would this be so? Candidates who were standing against the person supported by the landowner would use all sorts of means to try and break the stranglehold the landed families had over the voters. Here for example, are details of the expenses of a candidate in the 1802 county election in Carmarthenshire, in which he unsuccessfully challenged the local land-owners' candidate. Why has all this money been spent and on whom?:

Source 150

... Expenses amounted to £15,690 4s. 2d. This sum included payments to innkeepers for 11,070 breakfasts, 36,901 dinners, 684 suppers, 25,275 gallons of ale, 11,068 bottles of spirits, 8,879 bottles of porter, 460 bottles of sherry, 509 bottles of cider, and eighteen guineas for milk punch. The charge for ribbons was £786, and the number of separate charges for horse hire was 4,521.

Source: Report of the Royal Commission on Land in Wales and Monmouthshire, 1896.

The Parliamentary Reform Act of 1832 did give some areas where there had been growth of population due to the development of industry, a Member of Parliament for the first time. This was the case in Merthyr Tydfil and another example was in Mid-Wales where as a result of the growth of the woollen industry, the developing towns of Llanidloes, Newtown and Welshpool became part of the Montgomery Boroughs Parliamentary constituency. How-ever, the benefits of this reform were only really felt by the rising middle-classes such as the ironmasters of Merthyr Tydfil. This was because the right to vote hardly increased at all. In Merthyr, for example, there were still only 502 people out of a population of some 27,000 who had the right to vote even after the Reform Act. The way in which the ironmasters and other industrialists benefitted was seen in the county of Glamorgan. After the Reform Act there were three Borough constituencies in the county—Merthyr Tydfil, Cardiff and Swansea—and in future these were nearly always represented by an industrialist as M.P. In the two county seats, one M.P. was usually an industrialist and the other a Landowner. The lack of political power of working people was of course one of the reasons which led to disturb-ances such as the Merthyr Rising of 1831 and the Rebecca Riots. It was also part of the reason why working people tried to form trade-unions, but, these bodies were quickly crushed due to the opposition of employers. This did not mean that working-class protest disappeared, however. As the newspaper report below shows, there were violent incidents in these years:

Source 151

"SCOTCH CATTLE—John James (otherwise Shoni Coal Tar), aged 33, John Griffiths, aged 19, William Jenkins, aged 31 and Thomas Jarman, aged 35, were indicted for a burglary in the house of Thomas Rees, in the parish of Bedwellty, on the night of the 5th of January last. Thomas Rees, the prosecutor, stated that he lived at the Rock, in the parish of Bedwellty; that on the night of the 5th of January he went to bed about eleven o'clock—In about an hour and a half, he was alarmed by his servant girl, Sarah Jenkins; he got up and went towards the head of the stairs, where he saw two men ascending, the foremost of whom carried a blazing curtain upon the end of a pole . . . Directly after witness had retreated into the servant's room, the door was burst open by a man with a pole, and with which he commenced beating witness till he cried out, "O God! Let me have my life;" . . . After the men were gone away, witness went to the landing-place, and at length succeeded in extinguishing the fire, which had been fed with gowns, curtains, coats and other clothes; —he afterwards went downstairs, and dis-covered that the windows had been smashed in, the outer gate and the door burst open, three chairs, a bureau, a chest of drawers, earthenware and other things, broken to pieces, and in several places were marks as if the violence had been done with a sledge. He had had an iron chest, which stood upon the landing-place upstairs; this he found in the middle of the room down stairs, with the top demolished. It had contained on the night before 136 sovereigns, bills on different banks

Source 175

Lord John Russell (the Home Secretary) acquiesced (agreed) in the demand by sending three policemen! These men, although brave, were not of the slightest use . . . but . . . their presence proved a source of great irritation to the Chartists, who directed all their animosity against them.

Source: E. Hamer, *Brief Account of The Chartist Outbreak At Llanidloes*, 1867.

Marsh decided now to swear-in some 300 Special Constables and by 29 April 1839 there was a strong belief in Llanidloes that he was about to arrest the local Chartist leaders. That night the three London policemen arrived in the town and took up residence at the Trewythen Arms. This news and the growing rumours that action was to be taken against them led to the Chartists holding a meeting at the 'Long Bridge' in the town on the morning of 30 April. The Source below describes the news that was brought to this meeting and the action then taken by the Chartists:

Source 176

Messengers from different directions . . . shouted out that three of their comrades had been arrested in front of the hotel (the Trewythen Arms) by the London police . . . An instantaneous disorderly rush was made towards the Trewythen Arms . . . This crowd, with their numbers swelled on the way, soon arrived in sight of the hotel, where they saw the police and special constables drawn up to receive them . . . They withdrew for a few moments to procure (get) whatever they could lay their hands on in the form of weapons— guns, staves, pikes . . . Both parties afterwards accused the other of commencing the fray . . . the mob set up a terrible shout, and pressed forward towards the door of the inn . . . The women followed . . . by throwing stones at every window . . . Guns were next fired through the door, which . . . was ultimately burst open. The mob quickly spread themselves . . . in search of their comrades, whom they found handcuffed in the kitchen . . . One of the policemen . . . was soon found . . . he was then most savagely abused . . . Two of the London policemen managed to escape into a hay-loft of a stable . . . but they were dreadfully beaten . . .

Source: E. Hamer, *Brief Account of the Chartist Outbreak at Llanidloes*, 1867.

Some of the Chartists later argued that the person who first attacked the doors of the Trewythen Arms, shouting 'Hurrah for the Chartists', was none other than T. E. Marsh. It also appears that very few of the crowd were actually Chartist supporters—most were teenage labourers, housewives and known troublemakers in the town. Why might they have joined in? Nevertheless it was now the Chartists, under the leadership of Thomas Powell, who had control of Llanidloes.

The way they used this power is described below. Why would they have acted like this? What does this suggest on whether the Chartists had planned the attack on the Trewythen Arms?

Source 177

The Chartist leaders now became solicitous (concerned) about preserving order . . . in order to obtain the confidence of their fellow-townsmen . . . they appointed a few of their number to act as watchmen, whose duty it was to patrol the streets at night for the purpose of maintaining order.

Source: E. Hamer, *Brief Account of the Chartist Outbreak At Llanidloes*, 1867.

Marsh was still determined to take action against the Chartists, however, and he again requested the Home Secretary to send military assistance. This was now granted and troops arrived in the town on Saturday 3 May. Their arrival and the flight of the local Chartists is described below:

Source 178

. . . To the great joy of the people, a portion of the 14th regiment of light infantry . . . arrived from Brecon . . . Shortly afterwards, the cavalry rode into the town with drawn swords . . . The Chartists . . . abandoned all thoughts of organised resistance . . . Some scores . . . left the town in the course of the afternoon for south Wales—the iron works being regarded by them as the safest hiding place . . . On Monday morning . . . special constables . . . police and military . . . searched the houses of suspected persons . . . Four, who were implicated in the riot, were captured in this way . . . but the principal ringleaders had left . . .

Source: E. Hamer, *Brief Account of The Chartist Outbreak At Llanidloes*, 1867.

It seems that the military were surprised to find how little disorder there was in the town, compared with the reports they had received from Marsh and other magistrates. Although order was now completely restored and Marsh seems to have achieved his object of driving the Chartist leaders out of Llanidloes, no chances were taken (as the order banning further drilling by Chartists, p. 73, shows) and the reward notice which follows shows that the authorities were still determined to take action against the Chartists:

Source 179

HER MAJESTY'S PROCLAMATION

Victoria Regina.

Whereas, we have been given to understand that in some parts of our kingdom persons have of late unlawfully assembled together for the purpose of training and drilling persons to the use of arms, or of being trained or drilled for the purpose of practising military exercise, movements, or evolutions; and whereas the said assemblings and proceeding are prohibited by law, being dangerous to the peace and security of our liege subjects and of our authority, all persons guilty of such offences are punishable by transportation or imprisonment.

We therefore being duly sensible of the mischievous consequences likely to arise from such unlawful practices, if suffered to continue unpunished, and being firmly resolved to put the laws in execution for the punishment of such offenders, have thought fit by the advice of our Privy Council to issue this proclamation, hereby strictly commanding all Justices of the Peace, Sheriffs, Under Sheriffs, and all the Civil Officers whatsoever, that they do use their utmost endeavours to discover, apprehend, and bring to justice the persons concerned in the unlawful proceedings above mentioned.

And whereas, in some parts of our kingdom large numbers have lately assembled and met together, being armed with bludgeons and others offensive weapons, and have by their exciting to breaches of the peace, and by their riotous proceedings caused great alarm to our subjects; We therefore hereby strictly command all Justices of the Peace, Sheriffs and Under Sheriffs, and all other Civil Officers whatsoever, that they use their utmost endeavours to enforce the law, and proceed to put down and suppress such unlawful meetings and bring the offenders to justice. And we strictly enjoin all our liege subjects to give prompt and effectual assistance to our Justices of the Peace, Sheriffs and Under Sheriffs, and all other Civil Officers in their endeavours to preserve the public peace.

Given at our Court at Buckingham Palace, this 3rd day of May in the year of our Lord 1839, and in the second year of our reign.

God Save the Queen.

Source: E. Hamer, *Brief Account of The Chartist Outbreak at Llanidloes*, 1867.

Source 180

By Her Majesty's Command

£150 Reward!!!

Whereas Thomas Jarman, late of Llanidloes, carpenter, was apprehended at Llanidloes on 30th of April last, on a charge of FELONY, and rescued by a Mob and HATH SINCE ABSCONDED AND WHEREAS DAVID JENKIN HUGHES, late of Llanidloes, Printer, and ABRAHAM OWEN, of the same place,

Weaver, both absconded to avoid apprehension for the offence of unlawfully training and drilling to Arms.

Source: Glamorgan, Monmouth and Brecon Gazette, 25th May 1839.

Among the 32 local Chartists who were eventually arrested and imprisoned to await trial, was Thomas Powell. He was charged with making a seditious speech at Newtown at the beginning of April 1839. Of the others many were from Newtown and had no connection with the events which had taken place at Llanidloes. What does this suggest? The trial of these men began at Montgomery Assizes on 15 July, where they were defended by Hugh Williams. No proof was offered by the prosecution that the Chartists had planned the attack on the Trewythen Arms. Even someone who was opposed to the Chartists admitted this:

Source 181

Some of their papers were discovered . . . It was evidence . . . that they did not intend to commit any open acts of outrage against the authorities until a much later period than that of the riot, into which they had been led by the excitement arising from the unexpected arrest of three of their prominent men . . .

Source: E. Hamer, *Brief Account of The Chartist Outbreak at Llanidloes,* 1867.

Nevertheless all the Chartists were found guilty and they received harsh sentences as an example. The details of these sentences are shown below and this Source also supplies more information on the alleged activities of the Chartists and the charges brought against them:

Source 182

James Morris, for stabbing, with intent to do bodily harm, fifteen years transportation. John Ingram, Abraham Owen and Lewis Humphreys, for training and drilling to use arms, seven years transportation. John Evans (Tailor), John Lewis (Tatw), and John Lewis (Cripplegate), for riot and assault, twelve months imprisonment with hard labour. John Davies, Evan Pugh, Richard Owen, Isaac Lewis and Thomas Morgan, for training and drilling, six months imprisonment with hard labour. Joseph Jenkins, William Owen, John Evans (junior), Edward George, John Jones (Bel), William Jones (Fowler), James Jenkins, Daniel Jarman, David Morris, Thomas Morgan, Giles Richards, William Richards, Valentine Rowlands, Richard Thomas, Elizabeth Lucas, Margaret Meredith and Ann Williams, for riot, six months imprisonment

Social Conditions and Protest

Most of the workers in the developing industries of Monmouthshire had moved into the county from outside, in the search for work. This contributed to a rapid growth of population in areas of the county such as those below:

Source 188

Parish	1801 Population	1841 Population
Gelligaer	1,051	3,215
Bedwellty	1,434	22,413
Aber	805	11,272
Mynydd-islwyn	1,544	5,385
Llangynidr	775	2,775
Trevethin	1,472	14,942

Source: Population Figures for Monmouthshire Parishes taken from 1801 and 1841 Census of Population.

The difficulties which occurred because of such a rapid pace of development are shown in the source below which deals with housing and public health:

Source 189

The people are for the most part collected together in masses of from 4,000 to 10,000. Their houses are ranged round the works in rows... They rarely contain less than from one to six lodgers in addition to the members of the family . . . It is not unusual to find that 10 individuals of various ages and sex occupy three beds in two small rooms . . . The surface of the soil around is frequently blackened with coal, or covered with high mounds of refuse . . . The road . . . is often, in wet weather, ankle deep in black mud . . . Gardens are few . . . Due attention to sewerage is also overlooked . . .

Source: Report by Seymour Tremenheere on Housing Conditions in South Wales. *Minutes of the Committee of the Council on Education*, 1839-1840.

Despite the fact that a law of 1831 had made them illegal, Truck Shops continued to exist in the Monmouthshire iron towns and colliery villages, and they were a further grievance felt by workers. Due to frequent depressions in the iron and coal industries, there were often periods of unemployment and poverty for the industrial workers. The new Poor Law of 1834 was disliked as much in Monmouthshire as it was in west and mid-Wales. Evidence on the standard of living of people who did have work can be seen by comparing the household budgets given below, with the details of wages presented earlier in Source 187:

Source 190

Commodity	Price	Expenditure per month Collier	Furnaceman
Rent		Nil	Nil
Flour	13s 6d/bushel	£2 0s 6d	£2 0s 6d
Butter	1s/pound	8s 0d	12s 0d
Sugar	8d/pound	5s 4d	6s 8d
Tea	6d/pound	3s 9d	4s 6d
Cheese	7½d/pound	6s 3d	3s 9d
Bacon or ham	8d/pound	5s 4d	8s 0d
Fresh meat	7d/pound	11s 8d	14s 0d
Potatoes*		6s 0d	Nil
Currants	10d/pound	5d	5d
Raisins	7d/pound	3d	3½d
Blue, starch, pepper, mustard, etc.		10d	10d
Soap	7d/pound	3s 6d	2s 4d
Clothes, shoes, etc.		16s 0d	18s 0d
Tobacco	5s 4d/pound	2s 8d	2s 8d
Malt	3s 1½d/pound	Nil	Nil
Beer		6s 0d	Nil
Candles (for house)	7d/pound	7d	7d
Candles (for work)	7d/pound	4s 8d	Nil
Gunpowder	6½d/pound	6s 6d	Nil
Total Expenditure		£6 8s 3d	£6 3s 11d
Wages		£6 10s 0d	£6 10s 0d
Balance		1s 9d	6s 1d

Source: Household Budgets in South Wales 1839, based on Evidence in S. Tremenheere, *Minutes of the Committee of the Council on Education 1839-1840*, and cited in I. Wilks, *South Wales and the Rising of 1839*, 1984.

Although housing, public health and social conditions were better in the newer colliery villages of the Monmouthshire valleys than they were in the older irontowns, in most respects both types of industrial communities were very similar. They were places where most of the population were industrial workers and with most of the employers not living locally, the only middle-class inhabitants were shopkeepers, doctors and solicitors and the agents who managed the mines and works. Public houses and beer shops were the centres of working-class social life (in Dukestown, Tredegar for example, there were 5 public houses and 28 beer shops in an area of only 151 houses). Most of the immigrants came into the area from rural Wales and were Welsh-speaking. There was little opportunity for education other than in the Sunday schools which the Nonconformist Chapels (which sprung up everywhere in the new industrial communities of Monmouthshire) provided. Working and social conditions were harsh but the communities did not accept them without occasional protest, however. The Merthyr rebels of 1831 had looked to their fellows in Monmouthshire to support their Rising, for the Monmouthshire ironworkers and colliers also had often been involved in protest. In 1822, for example, there was a serious strike by colliers

places la
publican
Member:
a week,
have joi
claims tl
seen in t

Sou

A po
join
acci
tran
sam
kno
his
hin

Sou
183

Part
Chartis
to have
to thei
women
well.

In Ap
Wales,
the Ch
packed
reporte

So

Vi
th
cl:
pe
"(
ar.
Sc
C.

Vinc
and at
was re

S
v
b
a
p
s
t
S
c

The
Vince
furthe
and tl
again

in Monmouthshire. The best known of these protests, however, are the activities of the Scotch Cattle, for it was here that their 'Black Domain' was centred. When such protests took place, the authorities found it difficult to control them, for there were only 20 paid policemen in the whole of the coalfield at the time and the nearest soldiers were in Brecon. This made south Wales one of the least protected areas in the whole of Britain and was probably part of the reason why working-class protests were so frequent. By 1839 there was a new tide of protest developing in the industrial towns and villages of Monmouthshire and one observer described its causes as follows:

Source 191

There is something more in hand with the people at the present time than a mere question of a rise or fall in wages. They feel the degradation of being bound by laws, oppressive and tyrannical . . . made by persons who know nothing of their condition and their wants. They have felt there is . . . no hope of any amelioration (reform) from a Parliament elected by you—the middle classes. They have been robbed of the fruits of their labour, and their poverty and misery laughed at . . . They have been slaves, and . . . they are determined to be so not much longer . . .

Source: Western Vindicator: 24 August 1839.

THE GROWTH OF CHARTISM IN MONMOUTHSHIRE

Monmouthshire Politics and the Origins of Chartism

One of the grievances of working people suggested in Source 191 was their lack of political power. Politics in Monmouthshire, as elsewhere in Wales, had long been dominated by great landowning families. In this case there were two such families—the Somersets (the Dukes of Beaufort) and the Morgans of Tredegar House in Newport. They controlled two county seats in the House of Commons and the Borough seat (covering the boroughs of Newport, Monmouth and Usk). The candidates they supported for these seats were rarely even opposed in elections. From 1816, however, a challenge to their power did develop in the towns of Newport and Monmouth. Three men led this challenge—the industrialists John Hodder Moggridge and Thomas Prothero and *John Frost* of Newport. Below is a portrait of Frost and an account of his background:

Source: John Frost. From R. G. Gammage, *A History of Chartism*, 1854.

Source 193

Mr. John Frost . . . is the son of humble, and strictly honest parents, John and Sara Frost, who kept the Royal Oak public-house, in Mill Street, Newport . . . At about sixteen years of age he was put apprentice to a tailor in Cardiff . . . On his return to Newport, in the year 1811, he commenced business as a tailor and draper . . . Henceforth he took an active part in the politics of Newport and carried on a paper war against his opponents . . .

Source: E. Dowling. *The Rise and Fall of Chartism in Monmouthshire*, 1840.

Frost was a Radical in politics and in 1823 he was imprisoned after a libel case was proved against him, for attacking his opponents. He was at the forefront of the campaign in Newport in support of the Reform Bill in 1831. Newport had developed very rapidly as a town and a port due to the development of the industrial valleys of Monmouthshire. Its population grew from 1,423 in 1801 to 13,766 by 1841, but it still did not have its own Member of Parliament. However, the 1831 General Election did see the beginning of a change in the politics of Newport and Monmouthshire. In the Borough seat the ironmaster Benjamin Hall defeated the Marquis of Worcester (the brother of the Duke of Beaufort) and in further elections in 1835 and

Source 218

Source: Trial of Newport Chartists. R. G. Gammage, *A History of the Chartist Movement*, 1854.

Source 219

MONMOUTHSHIRE
Special Commission,
JANUARY. 1840.

SENTENCES
Of the Prisoners,

Tried before The Right Honourable N. C. Tindal Knight, the Honorable Sir J. Parke, Knight, and the Honorable Sir J. Williams, Knight.

COLTHURST BATEMAN, ESQ, SHERIFF,

1 John Frost, aged 54, charged with the crime of high treason against our Sovereign Lady the Queen her crown and dignity.   Guilty, sentence deferred.
2 Charles Waters, 26, for high treason.   Guilty, sentence deferred.
3 John Partridge, aged 44, for divers acts of treason.   6 months imprisonment.
4 James Aust, 23, for divers acts of treason and sedition.   7 years transportation.
5 Thomas Davies, 33, for high Treason.   Guilty, sentence deferred.
6 John Rees, 40, for high treason.   7 years, Transportation.

7 Richard Benfield, 20, for high treason.   2 years Imprisonment
8 William Jones 30, for high treason.   Guilty, sentence deferred
9 Amy Meredith, 45, ⎱ For feloniously breaking open the house of
10 James Meredith 11, ⎰ John Jones, at Trevethin, and stealing a quantity
11 Thomas Keys, 29, of bread and cheese, and a cask, containing six gallons of beer.   Not tried.
12 Solomon Briton, 23, for high treason and sedition.   7 years-transportation.
13 William Williams, 29, for feloniously breaking open the house of John Lloyd, at Bedwelty and taking from Ann Walters a quantity of rum, and gin, and beer. 12. months hard labour
14 George George, 27, for high treason and sedition.   acquitted
15 Thomas Davis, 28, charged with having been riotously assembled with other persons unknown at Abercarne, and compelled G. Hitchings to join them for an illegal purpose 18 Months Imprisonment
16 George Turner, 37, for treason and sedition.   7 years Transportation.
17 William Shellard, 36, for high treason and sedition.   2 years Imprisonment
18 Edmund Edmunds, 34, for high treason and sedition.   18, Months Imprisonment.
19 Samuel Etheridge, 61, for high treason and sedition.   12 Months Imprisonment.
20 John Lewis Lewellin, 49, for sedition.   12 Months Imprisonment.
21 Jenkin Morgan, 40, for treason and sedition.   18 Months Imprisonment.
22 Evan Edwards, 24, for high treason and sedition.   12 Months hard labour.
23 Benjamin Richards, 41, for high treason and sedition.   Not Tried.
24 Thomas Llewellin, 44, for treason, and sedition.   Not Tried.
25 Thomas Morgan, 29, charged with having raised the house of William Adams, at Ebbw Vale, with other persons armed with guns, spears, &c, and compelled him to join them in an unlawful combination and confederacy.
26 Zephaniah Williams, aged 44, for high treason and sedition. Guilty, sentence deferred
27 Moses Horner, William Horner, Thomas Davies, For stealing one shot belt, and one dagger, the property of William Thomas, of Mynyddislwyn.   Not tried.
30 Thomas Edwards aged 22, William John Llewellin, aged 20, Job Harris, aged 25 and Joseph Coales, aged 24, For breaking open and entering the dwelling house of John Walters of Bedwelty and violently and unlawfully assaulting him,
34 Lewis Rowland, aged 32 for sedition.   Not tried.
35 John Owen, aged 20, for high treason
36 John Lovell aged 41, for high treason and sedition.
37 John Batten 18, for conspiring against the peace of our sovereign Lady the Queen
38 Isaac Phillips 18, for stealing a cleaver, the property of Charles Harris, of Machen
True bills was also found on Tuesday against Henry Harris Isaac Davis David Williams, Charles Bicknell, James Moore, William Hotford, and Thomas Ball, for conspiracy and riot.

Hearth, Printer, Monmouth,

Source: Poster 1840 showing Sentences in Chartist Trials. Newport Central Library.

Source 220

> And now doth nothing more remain, than that the Court pronounce (to all of us a most painful duty) the last sentence of the law, which is, that each of you, John Frost, Zephaniah Williams, and William Jones, be taken hence to the place from whence you came, and be thence drawn on a hurdle to the place of execution, and that each of you be there hanged by the neck until you be dead; and that afterwards the head of each of you shall be severed from his body, and the body of each divided into four quarters, shall be disposed of as her Majesty shall think fit. And may the Lord have mercy upon your souls.

Source: Judge's Sentence on John Frost, Zephaniah Williams and William Jones at Chartist Trials. E. Dowling, *The Rise and Fall of Chartism in Monmouthshire*, 1840.

A campaign developed all over Britain to have these sentences reduced and the Chartist threatened that further Risings would occur if the leaders were executed. The Authorities in South Wales, however, were determined to carry out the sentences. To begin with the Government supported them in this, but on 31 January 1840 the Cabinet suddenly decided to reduce the sentences to transportation for life. On 18 February the three Monmouthshire Chartist leaders began their journey to convict colonies in Australia—Williams and Jones never to return to Wales.

Chartism in Monmouthshire after Newport

John Frost returned eventually to Newport in 1856 after receiving a pardon. He found, in fact, that there was still a strong Chartist presence in the town and in the valleys of Monmouthshire, where he was given a hero's welcome. As was the case in mid-Wales, Chartism in Monmouthshire did not come either to its head, or its end in 1839. In 1842 Chartism revived in Newport and many of the valley towns and although it later declined there were further revivals in the late 1840s and in the 1850s. It was a different type of Chartism to that of 1839 in that it was far more peaceful and it never reached the strength of the movement which had developed in the period up to the Newport Rising. Nevertheless it would be totally wrong to see the events of 1839 as the end of the Chartist movement in the county.

4. Postscript

Because the events which took place at Llanidloes and Newport in 1839 were such dramatic incidents and because historians have written so much about them, the history of Chartism in Wales is often completely linked to these areas and that particular year. Also because both of these events involved violence, Chartism in Wales is often seen as being the 'physical force' variety of the movement. Whilst this account has also concentrated upon these two episodes (mainly because so much evidence is available upon them) it is important to realise that this is not the *total* picture of Chartist activity in Wales. Mid-Wales and Monmouthshire were not the only places in Wales where Chartism had support. Merthyr Tydfil, for example, was probably the area where Chartism had the greatest support and certainly became the main centre of Welsh Chartism after 1839. Chartism certainly did not disappear in Wales after 1839. Whilst it never regained the number of supporters it had in 1839, in mid-Wales, Monmouthshire and other parts of Wales it remained a mass movement. In 1840, the Chartists campaigned for a pardon for the Chartist prisoners and to raise money to support their families. In the same year at Merthyr, two Chartist newspapers *Utgorn Gymru* (The Trumpet of Wales) and the *Merthyr Advocate* were started. In 1841 at Merthyr a local Chartist leader, Morgan Williams, campaigned for some time as a Chartist candidate in the general election of that year, when Chartism also thrived in places such as Cardiff, Llantrisant and Monmouth. In 1842 the National Chartist movement decided to draw up another Petition in support of the Charter to be presented to Parliament. Chartism revived throughout Wales in support of the Petition. In Merthyr, for example 21,934 signatures in support of the Petition were gained (the fifth largest number in Britain) and here is an account of the Merthyr Petition being taken from the town:

Source 221

"A huge petition in favour of the 'People's Charter', was, on Monday week, carried in procession through the principal streets of Merthyr Tydfil, to the railway terminus, from whence it was taken in the care of Mr. Morgan Williams of Penrheolgerrig . . . to London for presentation. It measured about two feet in breadth and about a foot and a half in circumference. A large concourse of workmen and others accompanied the procession . . ."

Source: *The Merthyr Guardian.*

Parliament again rejected the Petition, however. This led to a Chartist Strike in many parts of Britain in 1842, which had support in south Wales—especially in Merthyr Tydfil. Thereafter Chartism declined nationally but it still did not disappear in Wales and there were revivals in 1848 (when the third petition was presented unsuccessfully to Parliament) and in the early 1850s. As an organised movement Chartism finally disappeared in 1858, but there were still active Chartists in Wales at this time. Even in 1868 during the famous General Election campaign in Merthyr Tydfil when Henry Richard, the Radical politician, defeated H. A. Bruce, a local magistrate and ironmaster, local Chartists campaigned for him.

Concentration on the events of 1839 also gives a distorted view of the tactics normally followed by Chartists in Wales. The mid-Wales Chartists were probably not directly involved in the violence used in Llanidloes, but certainly the Newport incident was planned as a violent uprising. In the main, however, Welsh Chartists were not supporters of 'physical force' methods. The Merthyr Chartists refused to join in the Newport march and in the main they always preferred 'moral force' methods. Most of the Chartist leaders in Wales were respectable, peaceable people who simply wished to have the right to have a voice and a part to play in politics. Many of them were strong Nonconformists who believed through education, temperance and other methods that the Authorities would be persuaded that working-people were fit to have a say in the government of the country.

To what extent were the Chartists successful? In 1861 in Merthyr Tydfil, for example, only 1.4% of the population had the right to vote. As none of the other demands of the Charter had been met by this time, it would be possible to conclude that in the short-term they were not successful. By 1918, however, all the Chartist points (except the demand for Annual Parliaments) had been met and the campaign the movement had waged must have played some part in this. Perhaps even more importantly, the significance is that Chartism had been the first mass working-class movement in Wales and in Britain.

FURTHER WORK ON THE EVIDENCE

1. Look carefully at Source 154 and then answer these questions:
   a. What type of Source is this?
   b. What would you need to know before you could use this as a reliable Source on why Chartism gained support in Wales?
   c. What is being argued in the eighth vers ballad?
   d. What do the expressions 'Sons of and 'Sons of Wallia' mean? ' important to understand such ex

2. Look at Source 161 and then questions:
   a. What was the difference be' 'weaving shops' in the n industry and why were places?
   b. Why were mills and weaving shops u. to the river in Newtown?
   c. Why were mills and weaving shops built close to each other?
   d. This diagram comes from a book on the history of the woollen industry in Wales published in 1969. What would you need to know before you could take this to be a reliable historical source?

3. Look at Sources 167 and 168 and then answer the following:
   a. Given that you know where both these Sources are taken from what else would you need to know before you could take them to be reliable evidence on conditions in Newtown?
   b. Source 167 lists various jobs in the woollen industry and the wages paid for doing them. What does 'carded by an engine boy' mean? What jobs mentioned would you need to have more evidence on to discover what was involved?
   c. Why do you think in Source 167 weavers are paid much more than other workers? Would all these wages be profit to the weaver? Explain your answer.
   d. Why do you think Source 168 is incomplete in the evidence it gives?
   e. What other evidence would you need before you could use Sources 167 and 168 to estimate what woollen workers spent their wages on?

4. Consider Source 173 and then answer these questions:
   a. Who is the 'Hetherington' referred to here?
   b. What was the kind of Chartism argued for by Hetherington called?
   c. Why were the leaders of Chartism in mid-Wales 'surprised' by this?
   d. What would you need to know about this Source before you could use it as an accurate record of what took place at this meeting? What other possible sources could you compare it with?

   e. This Source is taken from a pamphlet written by a man opposed to the Chartists. Is there any clue in the Source which suggests this? Explain your answer.

5. Look at Source 179 and then answer the questions below:
   a. What about this Source suggests it was an 'official' document?
   b. Do you think the people of mid-Wales would have understood what was said in this Source? Why do you think this Source was published? Write out in your own words what the first ᵣraph in this Source is saying.

6. ʾource 190 and then answer these
      think neither of these men spent ᵗt?
      ch man spend the greatest y on? What does this tell you
      difference between the two they spend on candles and plain your answer.
      greatest difference between the tw what they spend on food?
   e. Does . evidence allow you to make confident statements on what working-men in Monmouthshire earned and what they spent their wages on? Explain your answer.

7. Look at Source 194 and then consider the questions below:
   a. What was the 'Working Men's Association' referred to in this Source?
   b. What was 'the Reform' referred to?
   c. Why does John Frost criticise this 'Reform'?
   d. What does this poster tell you about who the Newport Chartists were trying to gain support from at this time?

8. Look carefully at Source 203 then answer these questions:
   a. What is meant by 'to stop the Mails' and why would this have been important to the Chartists?
   b. What is meant by the phrase 'so that the people in the North would know they have succeeded'?
   c. What would you need to know about this Source before using it as reliable evidence on what the Monmouthshire Chartists planned?
   d. What are you told about the Source of this evidence which could lead you to doubt its reliability on the plans of the Chartists?

9. Look at Source 214 and then answer these questions:
   a. What does this Source argue the Chartist attack on Newport should be called?
   b. Why does it argue that it should be called this?
   c. What would you need to know before you could take the view put forward in this Source to be reliable? What other types of source might help you to decide on this?

landlords and tenants which led to the evictions which were examined in Sources 247 and 249. The Land Commission pointed to this as follows:

Source 259

The immense majority of the tenant farmers in the country districts are Nonconformists . . . On the most typical estates in Wales, the Landlord and his family belong to the Established Church, while the bulk of the tenants belong to one or other of the Nonconformist organisations . . . This remarkable fact had a powerful influence in creating a marked divergence (difference) between the opinions of the landowning class and the mass of the people, in enlarging the social difference between class and class which to some extent would have existed in any case, and in emphasizing (stressing) the opposing interests of landlord and tenant.

Source: Royal Commission on Land in Wales and Monmouth, 1893.

The 'social differences' mentioned in this Source refer to the charges made against Landlords that as well as being different to their tenants in their religion and lifestyle, they were also different in that often they did not live on their estates (i.e. they were 'absentee landlords') and because they did not speak Welsh, the language of the vast majority of their tenants. In addition to this, whereas their tenants tended to be Liberal in politics, they tended to support the Conservatives. Landlords did not necessarily accept that such differences were the case. Many of the Landlords of north-east Wales were thoroughly Welsh in origin and certainly they were not 'absentees' in comparison with landlords in Ireland. Nor did they accept that they were unsympathetic to their tenants. For example, J. E. Vincent argues below that the Church (which so many of the landlords belonged to) had changed its attitudes to the mass of people:

Source 260

I am far from saying that Denbighshire is at present free from clergymen who neglect their duties . . . but on the whole, there can be very little doubt that improvement in the Church has been prodigious (great) of late. Welsh services have been largely increased in number; mission halls and chapels have been erected . . . candidates for ordination (becoming clergymen) are compelled to pass a stringent examination in Welsh . . .

Source: J. E. Vincent, Letters from Wales, 1889.

Historians of Wales now argue that whilst there were obvious differences between landlords and their tenants, of themselves these did not lead to the hostility often shown by tenants towards landowners. These historians point to evidence of Liberal politicians and Nonconformist leaders using such differences to build up political campaigns in which landlords were blamed for all their tenants' problems. Below is an example of such an attack on landlords made by Thomas Gee in his newspaper. The strength of its language takes us to the heart of what really made up 'The Land Question':

Source 261

It is almost as difficult to get hold of a white rook in Wales, or a white elephant in Bengal, as it is to find a kind landlord. It is necessary for a man to walk scores of miles over hills and vales, through the wilderness and the forests, past many a village and hamlet, before he will see the cheerful face of one of these characters . . . The common idea of a landlord is a man who has the mouth of a hog, the teeth of a lion, the nails of a bear, the hoofs of an ass, the sting of a serpent, and the greed of the grave . . . The landowners of our country are, in general, cruel, unreasonable, unfeeling and unpitying men . . . Many of them have been about the most presumptuous (arrogant) thieves that have ever breathed . . .

Source: Baner ac Amserau Cymru, 2 November, 1887.

3. The Tithe Question

TITHES AND THE TITHE CAMPAIGN

By the 1880s all the various grievances seemed to come together in a campaign against another great source of complaint, the payment of tithes. In north-east Wales organised protests against the payment of tithes took place and from 1886 to 1891 a number of violent incidents occurred. These incidents reminded the Welsh Land Commissioners in 1893 of the Rebecca Riots (in fact the Tithe War has been called 'The Rebecca Riots of North Wales'). In this extract from their Report they explain why:

> Source 262
>
> In one sense, the anti-tithe movement was the Rebecca riots over again, but this time in North Wales. During the distress of the forties, the South Wales farmers found it easier to relieve themselves of the payment of the turnpike tolls than of rates or rent; the unpopular gatekeeper was more easily combated (fought) than the rate-collector or landlord. In 1885-88, the north Wales farmers regarded the tithe and the tithe-owners in much the same way as the turnpike toll and the gate-keeper had been regarded by their South Wales brethren a generation previously. They could not relieve themselves of a portion of the rent, their landlords were too strong for them, but the ordinary tithe owner was less able to fight them, and, moreover, payment of tithe had been always, more or less, unpopular with the bulk of people.
>
> *Source:* D. Ll. Thomas, *The Welsh Land Commission: A Digest of Its Report,* 1896.

Tithes

There are no such things as tithes in this country today. They were finally abolished by Parliament in 1936. Their history before then is a long one. The payment of tithes is mentioned in the Old Testament and with the development of the Christian Church they spread throughout Europe. It was not until 900, however, that the payment of tithes became law in England. Clergymen were to be supported by their parishioners by being paid a tithe (a tenth) of the produce of the land each year. These payments were 'in kind'. This meant presenting to the local vicar a share of crops (known as 'great tithes') and of animals (known as 'small tithes'). It was not only farmers who had to pay tithes: people who earned wages or who made profits from their work, were also liable to pay their share. The amount of tithes due from each person was

decided by officials known as Tithe Commissioners.

Tithes were not introduced into Wales until the 12th century with the conquest of the Normans. The payment of tithes was never very popular in Wales, but people usually paid up. After the setting up of the Church of England in the 16th century, following the break with the Roman Catholic Church, changes took place in the payment of tithes. During the reign of Henry VIII (1509-1547), a large number of monasteries were closed down and the rights which these monasteries had enjoyed to receive tithes were taken over by local gentry, who bought up large amounts of land which the monasteries had previously owned. Tenant farmers on these lands now had to pay their tithes to their new landlords, who were still expected to pay over these tithes to the local clergy. However, in many cases landlords paid very little, if anything, to the clergy. This was often the reason why in many cases local churches in Wales had little wealth. It became the case that the tithes—which people probably had never liked paying—were often now not even being paid for the purpose intended but were another payment to landlords.

By the 19th century the payment of tithes had become even more unpopular in Wales as the majority of people were not members of the Church of England. The Source below (written by a Nonconformist Minister) explains what objection this led to:

> Source 263
>
> Is it not unjust to compel Independents, Methodists, Baptists, Wesleyans, Unitarians etc. to contribute towards the support of the Clergy of the Church of England . . . Welsh tithes are taken out of the country to swell the revenues of English bishops, cathedral bodies and colleges. The Bishop of Lichfield thus takes the whole of the tithe of Pennal, £223; Talyllyn, £250; and Towyn, £293 in value.
>
> *Source:* Rev. W. Thomas, *The Anti-Tithe Movement in Wales,* 1891.

In 1836 further changes in the payment of tithes were made when Parliament passed the *Tithe Commutation Act.* This allowed tithes to be paid in money instead of 'in kind'. The amount to be paid each year by individuals would remain the same for a certain period of time. This charge was decided by averageing out the price received by farmers for their wheat, barley and oats, over a seven year

The 'Tithe War' Spreads

In the autumn and early winter of 1886 similar protests to the one at Llanarmon, spread throughout the Vale of Clwyd and north-west Flintshire. At *Whitford*, for example, in December 1886, a crowd of a thousand or so farmers gathered to protest against a distraint sale, and again eighty policemen were needed to protect the auctioneer. This did not prevent at attack being made upon them, as the Deputy Chief Constable of Flintshire describes below:

Source 271

The auctioneer was hit very frequently and so was I; but I did not mind that very much, as it was done partly in good humour. At this point a rush was made to force myself and the auctioneer down to the horse-pond. A hole had been made in the ice, and evidently the intention was to get us through. We, however, got away without anything more serious than being pelted with snowballs and rotten eggs.

Source: Evidence of Deputy Chief Constable Bolton of Flintshire Constabulary to Committee of Enquiry Into the Tithe Agitation in Wales, 1887.

Such incidents continued into 1887. In June 1887 a serious disturbance took place at *Mochdre* when the Riot Act was read and eighty-four people (thirty-four of whom were policemen) were seriously injured. Below is a newspaper report of this event and it is followed by evidence from the Chief Constable of Denbigh on the attack made on the police:

Source 272

On Thursday morning, a large force of police, numbering upwards of 100 men, drafted from the Flintshire and Denbighshire forces, assembled at the General Railway Station, Chester, where they were joined by a full company of the 22nd Cheshire Regiment . . . (They travelled by special train) . . . to Mochdre, a small village about 1½ miles from Colwyn Bay. So the train pulled up at the crossing, and the uniform of the military were observed from a look-out post, which was the highest point of the adjacent mountain range which had been occupied from daybreak to dusk for a full week, a number of cannon were fired, and a big flag hoisted on a flagstaff. The discharge of the cannons was the signal to the farmers and peasantry in the surrounding locality. A number of people could almost immediately be observed coming in all directions to the point at which the military were mustering prior to marching to Mynydd Mochdre, a farm lying up on the hills about 2 miles from the railway crossing . . . and at the farm the tenant, a Mr. Hugh Roberts, declined

to pay the amount of his tithe, £6-14-7d., for which act one cow had been distrained upon . . . A start was made for the field in which the cow was . . . By this time the crowd from the hills were reinforced by large numbers coming from Colwyn Bay and other adjacent towns. The mob became more and more unruly, and the auctioneer was subjected to all manner of insult. The road was blocked, and the crowd refused to move, the police were compelled to force a passage, in which they were somewhat roughly used, stones being thrown from the rear. The police drew their truncheons for a few moments, and charged the mob right and left. About a dozen were carried out in an insensible condition. One man, Elias Hughes, a deacon in a chapel in the locality, who had been particularly active in the anti-tithe movement, was badly injured, his skull being cracked and his arm broken. After the police charge the money was immediately paid, and the police moved on. Suddenly a shower of huge stones was hurled with great force from behind hedges. Another attack was made, this time in right earnest. The crowd scattered like rabbits, the police following them up the hill . . . The Riot Act was read both in English and Welsh . . . Several policemen were injured but only one seriously.

Source: The Flintshire Observer, 23 June, 1887.

Source 273

. . . plastered all over the head with cowdung . . . I felt a pressure all around me, of being pushed down violently by the crowd. At that moment I saw stones coming from the field on my right into the ranks of the police . . . I saw sticks and staves in use one moment . . . First of all I saw the pressure of the rear of the police. Then I saw the police endeavouring to keep back the crowd, but to begin with, I saw the cowdung.

Source: Evidence of Chief Constable Leadbetter of Denbighshire to Committee of Enquiry into the Tithe Agitation in Wales, 1887.

Llangwm and the Widening Outbreaks

Up to this time the spread of the 'Tithe War' had not led to any arrests, but events at *Llangwm* in September 1887 were to change this. Here again the refusal to pay tithes was followed by distraints and an auction was arranged. A police inspector and twenty-four policemen accompanied the auctioneer as he tried to sell two cows! No one was prepared to make a bid for the cows and the crowd pelted the auctioneer and police with rotten eggs. Eventually order was restored and the cows were sold to a Rhyl butcher whom the auctioneer had brought with him! The local farmers, however, blocked all the roads from the village and prevented the cows from being removed. Two days later a new auction was held, but again there was uproar and the crowd eventually drove the auctioneer and policemen out of the village. Thirty-one people were summoned for their part in this incident and eventually eight of these were brought to trial at Ruthin Assizes in February 1888. They were charged with assault and riot and found guilty. The Judge, however, stated that he believed they had been encouraged by others to act as they did and they were only bound over to keep the peace in the sum of £20 each. These men became known as 'The Llangwm Tithe Martyrs' and those who were summoned are shown below:

Source 274

Source: The Llangwm Tithe Martyrs, July 1887. Clwyd Record Office.

By this time the tithe disturbances were spreading out of north-east Wales across the borders into the neighbouring counties of *Caernarfonshire* (where in 1886 the young David Lloyd George was heavily involved in organising anti-tithe meetings) and *Montgomeryshire*. In 1889 some incidents even occurred in Rebecca's old home in Cardiganshire and Pembrokeshire. In Denbighshire and Flintshire in 1888 the Church decided to make a greater effort to raise the tithes by force. By now, however, the Anti-Tithe leaders had decided to use more peaceful protest tactics. Therefore, although there were still many cases of distraint there were very few violent disturbances. There was one major exception to this, however, and it took place at *Llannefydd* in Denbighshire in May 1888. Police had been used for some time in this area to protect tithe collectors, but on 10 May only two officers accompanied a collector who was visiting farms in the Llannefydd area. Soon a crowd of farmers gathered to follow them and after visiting only four farms, the crowd drove

them back into Denbigh. A week later eleven policemen were used to protect the tithe collectors and a new attempt was made to visit the farms. After visiting ten farms they were again forced to retreat by a hostile crowd. Next day the Chief Constable, a Superintendent and thirty-two officers gave protection, but to no avail as there was a violent clash with farmers in which twenty-five people were injured. Here is a description of events on that day:

Source 275

Men were knocked down without the slightest provocation. Blood was to be seen streaming on all sides. Men were lying down on the road insensible . . . All were suffering from ghastly scalp wounds, and many suffered keenly from the loss of blood. The sight of some of the wounded was awful. The blood flowed in such a proportion from the top of their heads till it congealed on their necks, face, and shoulders, presenting a sickening appearance.

Source: Denbigh County Herald, 18 May 1888.

The Chief Constable of Denbigh decided to ask for military assistance and a troop of the *9th Lancers* were sent to the area. For the next month they helped the police protect tithe collectors carrying out their work. Source 276, p. 110, shows the Cavalry in Denbigh and it is followed (Source 277) by an illustration showing some of the incidents which took place in the area at this time.

An Overview of 'The Tithe War'

There were further tithe protests in 1889 and 1890 and some isolated incidents after this time. However, by 1891, the 'Tithe War' had really come to an end and it died away almost as suddenly as it had first flared up in 1886. To what extent had the 'Tithe War' been a planned campaign? One thing that was not planned was the level of violence. As well as the disturbances at auctions and when tithe collectors were doing their work, there were other violent incidents. Threatening letters were sent to Church of England clergymen and in some cases (at Bodfari in Flintshire, for example) the homes of parsons were attacked. J. E. Vincent claims below that farmers were often terrorized into supporting the tithe campaign:

Source 278

The farmers who would like to pay . . . go in fear of social boycotting (being isolated by their fellow farmers). They are afraid that their

Source 276

Source: Troops in Denbigh, May 1888. Clwyd Record Office.

Source 277

Source: The Tithe Disturbances at Denbigh, *Daily Graphic*, August 1890.

fellows will show them the cold shoulder in the market-place . . . or that some desperate character will fire their ricks; and it must be remembered that in a small community like that which exists in the Vale of Clwyd a few reckless scoundrels are capable of exercising a strong terrorizing influence.

Source: J. E. Vincent. *Letters From Wales,* 1889.

This level of violence was not planned by, or part of the policy of, the Land League and the Anti-Tithe groups. The Welsh Land Commission in 1893 was to state that, in its view, the violence was the result of the frustration of farmers who had faced a long depression in agriculture. What was quite clearly planned, however, was the campaign against tithe payment. Here the Land League and Thomas Gee were to the fore. Below Thomas Gee sets out the Land League's viewpoint:

Source 279

The tithe is not a tax upon the land, but upon its produce, and thereby upon the brains, the capital, and the industry of the tenant farmer. He has the option, according to law, of paying his tithe either voluntarily or by distraint.

Source: Baner Ac Amserau Cymru, 21 December, 1887.

By encouraging as many farmers as possible not to pay tithes, thereby forcing the authorities to raise the tithe through distraint and auctions Gee and his supporters achieved two things. In the first place the whole system of collecting tithes was put to the test and found to be unworkable. The authorities were having to spend more money on collecting the tithes, through having to employ bailiffs, auctioneers and policemen, than was actually received from the tithe! Secondly, the campaign gave tremendous publicity to the opposition which tenant farmers had to the tithes and to the 'Land Question' as a whole. Below is a photograph of Thomas Gee on his horse 'Degwm' (Tithe) and this is followed by evidence from the Land Commission of 1893 on the activities of the Welsh Land League in the tithe campaign:

Source 280

Source: Thomas Gee on his horse 'Degwm'. Clwyd Record Office.

Source 281

The League . . . in its report for 1888 . . . stated that since the formation of the League . . . about 300 farmers who were members, have had their stock distrained upon, and many actual sales have taken place . . . but all the losses which have been suffered, and all the costs which have been incurred, have been paid in full, including the cost of solicitors for attending sales.
Source: D. Ll. Thomas. *The Welsh Land Commission: A Digest of its Report*, 1896.

As could be expected the Tithe campaign met with different reactions from those in authority. Welsh Liberal M.P.s gave some support to the campaign. However, whilst they protested in Parliament over the action of the police at Mochdre in June 1887, they also made plain their dislike of the more violent episodes

of 'the Tithe War'. Landlords saw the attack on tithes as being part of the wider campaign against them being fought by the leaders of Nonconformity. Some Landlords hit back by evicting tenants who refused to pay tithes. The local authorities in Denbighshire and Flintshire acted with a great deal of restraint and very few arrests were made during the period. The reason for this is suggested below by J. E. Vincent—what is he arguing for here?

Source 282

In Denbighshire there is an almost universal consensus (general agreement) of opinion among law-abiding persons to the effect that peace cannot be restored by anything short of either disestablishment or a measure casting the tithes, in the first instance, upon the shoulders of the landowner.
Source: J. E. Vincent, *Letters From Wales*, 1889.

Vincent's final point in Source 283 was supported by Mr. John Bridge, who was appointed by the Home Secretary to enquire into the Tithe disturbances after the Mochdre incident in 1887. In 1891 an Act *'To Make Better Provision for the Recovery of Tithe Rentcharge'* was passed by Parliament and tithes now had to be paid to the Church by Landlords rather than by the tenant farmers. Whilst this meant that Nonconformist tenant farmers no longer had to pay to a Church they did not belong to, it did not completely overcome their grievance against the tithes. Most landowners increased tenants' rents to cover the tithe payment and in some cases where tenants refused to pay rents raised for this reason, they were evicted. 'The Land Question' was now fully directed against the landlords rather than the Landlords and the Church, as before. Thomas Gee and his supporters began to accept that their religious objection to tithes could only finally be settled by the Church becoming *disestablished*—that is no longer being the 'official' Church of the Welsh people. The Land League after 1888 began to campaign for Disestablishment and wider issues of 'the Land Question', as well as over Tithes. These two factors—the 1891 Act and the change in tactics of the Land League—largely explain the end of the 'Tithe War' in 1891.

4. Conclusion

In 1920, the Church was Disestablished in Wales by Act of Parliament. However, this did not bring an end to tithes which continued to be paid until they were finally abolished in 1936. The issue of tithe payment had long before this, however, been overtaken by the wider issues of 'the Land Question' in Wales. Historians now argue that whilst landlords were unfairly blamed for the poor state of Welsh agriculture in the late nineteenth century, there is no doubt that the majority of tenant farmers in Wales had lost sympathy for their landlords and were becoming increasingly bitterly opposed to them. There were many reasons for this and these divisions were played up by Nonconformist leaders such as Thomas Gee and Liberal politicians such as Thomas Ellis and David Lloyd George. However, there was also a strong feeling among tenant farmers that whilst economically they were poor, their landlords grew even richer. The Welsh Land Commission of 1893, which inquired into the causes of the 'Land Question' in Wales, found that the position was as follows in Source 283:

Source 283
The Commissioners express the opinion that in Wales it is the tenant farming class that have hitherto borne the brunt of depression. In the majority of cases the tenant has during recent years, found it increasingly difficult to pay his rent . . . Many tenant farmers have failed completely . . . a very large number will shortly be face to face with the prospect of bankruptcy . . . Next to the tenant farmers, the landowners of the country have suffered most . . . The estate owners of Wales have naturally lived . . . in a way that has . . . left little or no margin . . . But though this is the case, there is, so far . . . no sign . . . that the landowning class . . . is in a position of embarrassment.
Source: Report of the Royal Commission on Land in Wales and Monmouth, 1896.

After the 1914-1918 War the predictions of the Land Commission were shown to be wrong as far as the position of landowners were concerned. Many landowners were now to find themselves in debt and increasingly the great landed estates of Wales were sold off. The figures below show that it was the tenant farmers of Wales who now bought and owned the land that they already farmed:

Source 284

PERCENTAGE OF HOLDINGS OWNED BY OCCUPIER

	1887[127]	1909[128]	1941—43[129]	1960[130]	1970[131]
Anglesey	5.1	12.08	30	48.2	54.5
Breconshire	9.4	9.37	44	60.0	64.2
Cardiganshire	21.6	18.53	48	71.4	72.0
Carmarthenshire	11.3	11.57	42	53.4	68.2
Caernarfonshire	4.2	11.66	30	48.8	58.4
Denbighshire	12.2	7.3	34	56.0	60.6
Flintshire	10.0	8.3	36	54.9	58.3
Glamorgan	9.1	6.02	24	52.9	57.6
Merioneth	7.5	7.09	25	48.3	58.6
Monmouthshire	13.8	12.84	33	61.0	64.2
Montgomeryshire	6.8	8.47	48	64.5	66.8
Pembrokeshire	10.3	10.53	36	57.7	64.2
Radnorshire	15.7	13.49	40	62.3	67.5
Wales	10.5	10.58	37	58.4	63.7

Source: J. Davies. 'The End of the Great Estates and the Rise of Freehold Farming in Wales', *The Welsh History Review.*

With this development came the end of the so called 'Land Question' in Wales. For much of the nineteenth century it had been extremely important in the life of rural Wales and had led to many protests. 'The Tithe War' in Denbighshire and Flintshire in the 1880s was one of the most important of such protests.

FURTHER WORK ON THE EVIDENCE

1. Look carefully at Sources 223, 236 and 237 and then answer the following questions:
   a. Compare what Sources 223 and 237 have to say about the diet of people in rural areas.
   b. Compare what Sources 223 and 236 reveal about housing conditions in rural areas at this time.
   c. What information does Source 223 provide which Sources 236 and 237 do not?
   d. Do you think that all of these Sources are reliable? Explain your answer.

2. Look at Sources 223 and 234 and then answer the questions below:
   a. What evidence do these Sources provide on agricultural work at this time?
   b. What would you need to know before you could accept these Sources as reliable evidence on agricultural work during this period? What other types of evidence would help you to check this reliability.
   c. Look back to earlier sources in this book and compare with Source 233 and 234. What conclusions can you arrive at on work in industry in Wales in the 19th century compared to work in agriculture?

3. Look at Sources 243 and 244 and then consider these questions:
   a. What does Henry Richard mean in Source 243 when he says 'the people of Wales have never yet been represented in the House of Commons'? What evidence does he give to explain why this was so?
   b. What might make you doubt the reliability of Source 243. What other evidence would help you to test the reliability of this Source?
   c. What major change in Welsh politics is shown in Source 244? Use the numerical evidence in the Source to help explain your answer.
   d. What major reforms made the changes shown in Source 244 possible?

4. Look carefully at Source 246 and with the help of other Sources, answer the questions below:
   a. What does T. E. Ellis mean when he says that tenants have been evicted 'for exercising independent judgement in politics'? What light do Sources 247 and 248 throw on his claim?
   b. What does T. E. Ellis mean in Source 246 by his fifth point? What evidence do Sources 255 and 256 offer on this point?
   c. What in Source 246 does Ellis mean by his sixth point. How do Sources 257 and 258 throw further light on his claim?
   d. From what you have been told about T. E. Ellis and the information given in Source 246 what do you think are his strengths and weaknesses as a witness on 'the Land Question'?

5. Look at Source 251 and then answer the following questions:
   a. Why would it be important to Landowners that their tenants kept 'the house and all buildings, gates and fences' in good repair?
   b. Why would the Landlord here only allow his tenant to keep one dog?
   c. Why would an additional rent of £10 be charged for every extra acre the tenant farmed?
   d. Why might tenants have felt a grievance at having to do two days work annually for their Landlords?

6. Look at Source 254 and then consider these questions:
   a. What does the word 'tenement', used in the Source, mean?
   b. How many of the nineteen farmers listed have held their land for 10 years or more and how many for 50 years or more?
   c. How do you think the information in this Source was collected?
   d. What was the purpose of J. E. Vincent collecting this information?
   e. Why might the reliability of the information be questioned? How could its reliability be checked?

7. Look at Source 263 and then answer the following questions:
   a. Who were the 'Independents, Methodists, Baptists, Wesleyans, Unitarians'?
   b. What does the author of this Source particularly object to?
   c. What are you told about this Source which might make you question its reliability? Explain your answer.

8. Look carefully at Sources 266 and 267 and then answer the questions below:
   a. What reason does Source 266 give for the poor financial state of Welsh farmers?
   b. Explain the 'three planks' in the 'reform platform' mentioned in Source 266.
   c. What does Thomas Gee mean in Source 267 when he says that the state of agriculture is 'not the cause but the occasion of this agitation'?

9. Look at Source 269 and then consider these questions:
   a. What is meant by the phrase 'distrained upon'?
   b. What was distrained upon at each of the farms mentioned in this source?
   c. What is meant by saying that 'disestablishment . . . the only remedy'?

10. Look at Source 272 and then answer the following questions:
   a. What was the purpose of cannons being fired and a flag raised?
   b. What evidence is there here to show the involvement of Nonconformists in the Tithe protests?
   c. Compare what this Source has to say on how the riot started with what Source 273 has to say.

CONVERSION TABLE

Old Money to Decimals

It was in 1971 that the decimal coinage which we use today was introduced in Britain. Until then the value of our money was expressed in pounds, shillings and old pence (£.s.d.). Therefore most of the amounts of money mentioned in the Sources in this book are expressed in these old money values. To convert them into the decimal values of today you should use the figures below:

Old Pence/shillings/Pounds		New Pence
1 old penny	=	0.41 new pence
12 old pence or 1 shilling	=	5 new pence
240 old pence or 20 shillings or £1	=	100 new pence or £1

Price Equivalence

As we know all too well what our money is worth *today* (that is how much it can buy) will not be what it will be worth in a year's time. This is because of *inflation* which simply means that over a period of time the value of £1 will decrease as prices rise. Over a long period of time, such as the period of about 150 years which we have looked at in this book, there will be a great change therefore, in the value of money. Throughout this book the Sources include references to money, such as how much people earned and how much things cost to buy. To get some idea of what these figures mean we need to try and relate them to the value of our money today. This is not at all an easy thing to do and we have to be very careful with such calculations, therefore. However, one of our major banks has tried to do these calculations for the period 1883-1923 and its figures are set out overleaf. They should give you some help in making sense of what the various prices mentioned in the Sources actually mean in terms of our money today.

1883
£1 then	=	3½ today
1 shilling then	=	0.17p today
1 old pence then	=	0.014p today

1913
£1 then	=	3½ today
1 shilling then	=	0.17p today
1 old pence then	=	0.014p today

1923
£1 then	=	6p today
1 shilling then	=	0.3p today
1 old pence then	=	0.025p today

Glossary

Assizes — Courts where a High Court Judge and a Jury try serious offences.

Bailiffs — Officers employed by a Court to seize the property of people in debt, so that it could be sold to pay off those debts.

Bar Iron — Pig Iron which has been treated to remove impurities and then rolled into bars. Also called *wrought iron*.

Boroughs — Towns which had the right to govern themselves and (either by themselves or with other boroughs) to elect a Member of Parliament.

Census — An official count of the population of Britain usually held every ten years since 1801.

Cholera — An infectious and often deadly disease carried by bacteria in impure water.

Coke — Raw coal that has been baked to burn-off impurities so that it can be used for smelting purposes.

Common Land — Land used by the whole community for grazing animals, collecting firewood etc.

Constituencies — The area represented by a Member of Parliament.

Corn Laws — Laws passed by Parliament in 1815 stating that until the price of British corn reached 80 shillings a quarter, no corn could be imported.

Day Schools — Schools held during weekdays—so called to distinguish them from Sunday Schools.

Democracy — A system where the people who live in a country have some say in how it is governed—usually by choosing representatives in elections.

Disestablishment — The campaign fought by Nonconformists to stop the Church of England being the official (or 'established') Church in Wales.

Distraint — To seize goods from someone to pay off their debts.

Drilling — Exercise and training for soldiers.

Enclosures — The process whereby land owned by a person which is scattered around a village, or land which has not been used before for farming (such as Common Land) is brought together and enclosed by a fence, ditch or hedge.

Evictions — Where Landlords force their tenants to leave their property because of non-payment of rent or other reasons.

Felony — A serious crime such as murder or treason.

Flannel — Soft woollen cloth which was made a great deal in Wales.

Forges — Where pig iron was re-heated and hammered to remove impurities and to strengthen and shape it.

Freeholders — Farmers who held their land by right rather than renting it from a Landlord.

Friendly Societies — Organisations which collected regular contributions from members, which could be claimed back in times of illness, old-age and death by them or their families.

Fulling — The finishing process in making woollen cloth where, in a mill, water and fuller's earth was used to give the cloth a smooth, felt-like, finish.

Furnaces — Ovens where the raw materials needed to produce iron were heated and a liquid metal was produced.

Gentry — The well-born or privileged in society, who own land and usually hold titles.

Indicted — To be charged with an offence and be required to appear before a Judge and Jury to be tried on it.

Insurrection — An organized attempt to overthrow the Government of a country.

Improvements — The drainage of land, erecting new fences or buildings on it etc. To 'improve' its value.

Iron Ore — The rock containing the mineral iron which had to be heated to separate the metal from the rock. Also called *ironstone*.

Land Hunger — Where there are more people seeking to own or rent land than there is land available for them.

Leaseholders — People who hold land or other property for a certain period of time under a lease from the Landowner.

Levels — Tunnels driven from a hillside into seams of coal close to the surface.

Lime Kilns — Ovens where limestone is heated to turn it into lime powder for use as a fertilizer.

Lock-Out — Where employers refuse work to their employees who are not prepared to accept changes in their terms of employment such as wage cuts.

Looms — Machines worked by hand-power on which the weaving of woollen cloth was done.

Magistrates — Important members of the community (such as Landowners and Industrialists) who were appointed by the Crown to preserve law and order, catch law-breakers and try them where the offences were not very serious. They also helped to run local affairs by, for example, controlling the Poor Law. Also known as J.P.s (Justice of the Peace).

Master Weavers — Men who employ a number of weavers to supply them with woven woollen cloth.

Militia — A group of men who in an emergency take up arms to support the Government.

Nonconformists — Members of Chapels, i.e. of groups which had broken away from the Church of England and set up their own religious groups. Also known as *Dissenters*.

Parish	The area under the care of a clergyman of the Church of England and an area of local government.
Peck	A unit of measurement equal to about two gallons.
Petition	A way of people making their views known to the Monarch and Parliament.
Pig Iron	The liquid metal drained off from an iron furnace.
Poor Law	The system of laws under which people who were unable to work (through illness, old-age and other reasons) could apply for poor relief.
Poor Law Guardians	People elected by the ratepayers to run the Poor Law System. Guardians would decide how much money should be raised for poor relief and how it was distributed.
Radicalism	The political outlook held by people known as Radicals, who believed that widescale reforms were needed in Britain.
Sale-Coal	Coal which was sold on the open market rather than mined especially for use in Ironworks and other industries.
Sandstone	A rock made up of layers of sand which was used in house-building.
'Scotch Cattle'	A secret organisation of workers in South Wales which used violent methods to oppose Employers and against workers who 'Blacklegged' during strikes.
Smelting	The heating or melting of iron ore in a furnace to produce molten or liquid iron.
Special Constables	Men chosen by Magistrates to help them keep law and order. These men were part-time or only appointed for a particular period of time.
Spindles	Rods onto which thread is wound for spinning or weaving.
Tenant Farmers	Farmers who held their land as tenants, i.e. they did not own the land but leased it for a period of time from Landowners.
Tithe Commissioners	Officials who were responsible for deciding the level of tithes to be paid and for their collection.
Tollhouses	Places on a Turnpike Trust road where travellers had to pay a toll for using the road.
Transportation	Being sent to a convict colony in Australia and performing hard labour there as a punishment for being found guilty of an offence.
Turnpike Trusts	Bodies formed to build and improve roads. They charged a toll on travellers using these roads.
Unitarians	Members of a Nonconformist religious group who hold radical views on religion and politics.
Workhouses	Building set up under the Poor Law which people were made to enter if they were to receive poor relief after the 1834 Poor Law Amendment Act. Conditions in the Workhouses were made deliberately bad to discourage people from seeking poor relief unless they were desperate.

INDEX